VICTORIAN EXTERIOR DECORATION

ROGER W. MOSS AND **GAIL CASKEY WINKLER**

VICTORIAN EXTERIOR DECORATION

How to Paint
Your Nineteenth-Century
American House Historically

HENRY HOLT AND **COMPANY**   **NEW YORK**

ALSO BY ROGER W. MOSS AND GAIL CASKEY WINKLER

Victorian Interior Decoration: American Interiors 1830–1900

Copyright © 1987 by LCA Associates
All rights reserved, including the right to reproduce this
book or portions thereof in any form.
Published by Henry Holt and Company, Inc.,
115 West 18th Street, New York, New York 10011.
Published in Canada by Fitzhenry & Whiteside Limited,
91 Granton Drive, Richmond Hill, Ontario L4B 2N5.

Library of Congress Cataloging-in-Publication Data
Moss, Roger W.
Victorian exterior decoration.
1. Decoration and ornament, Architectural—United States.
2. Decoration and ornament, Victorian—United
States.   3. Color in architecture—United States.
I. Winkler, Gail Caskey.   II. Title.
NA3503.7.M68   1987   698'.12   86-15014

ISBN 0-8050-0376-2
ISBN 0-8050-2313-5 (An Owl Book: pbk.)

Henry Holt books are available at special discounts
for bulk purchases for sales promotions, premiums,
fund-raising, or educational use. Special editions or
book excerpts can also be created to specification.
For details contact: Director, Special Markets.

First published in hardcover by
Henry Holt and Company, Inc., in 1987.
First Owl Book Edition—1992

Designed by Kate Nichols
Printed in the United States of America
Recognizing the importance of preserving the written word,
Henry Holt and Company, Inc., by policy, prints all of its
first editions on acid-free paper. ∞

3   5   7   9   10   8   6   4   2

1   3   5   7   9   10   8   6   4   2
pbk.

CONTENTS

ACKNOWLEDGMENTS

In the course of preparing this book we have leaned heavily on friends and colleagues across the United States. Many of them are the owners of Victorian buildings with whom we have worked or who have shared their restoration joys and frustrations with us over the past decade. Unfortunately, we cannot acknowledge all of them here, but they know who they are and we thank them for contributing to what follows. For more specific help, we particularly want to mention James Bale, Devoe Paint Company, Louisville, Kentucky; our favorite Cape May, New Jersey, innkeepers, Tom and Sue Carroll, Jay and Marianne Schatz, and Joan and Dane Wells, for holding the line against "painted ladies"; Thomas P. Carll, Sherwin-Williams Paint Company, Cleveland, Ohio; Charles Carpenter, Glidden Paint Company, Cleveland, Ohio; H. Grant Dehart and Randolph Delehanty, San Francisco, California; Harry Devoe, Philadelphia, Pennsylvania; Hank Dunlop, San Francisco, California; Daniel P. Jordan, Thomas Jefferson Memorial Foundation, Inc., Charlottesville, Virginia; Cathy Klimaszewski, The 1890 House, Cortland, New York; Raymond H. Maier, City of Bridgeton, New Jersey; Lee H. Nelson, AIA, Department of the Interior, Washington, D.C.; Leslie C. O'Malley, Cortland County Historical Society, Cortland, New York; Ellie Reichlin, Society for the Preservation of New England Antiquities, Boston, Massachusetts; Jay Ruby, editor, *Studies in Visual Communication*, Philadelphia, Pennsylvania; Paul D. Schweizer, Munson-Williams-Proctor Institute, Utica, New York; Arlene Palmer Schwind, Victoria Society of Maine, Portland, Maine; Guy Lacy Schless, president, the Victorian Society in America, Philadelphia, Pennsylvania, for permission to quote from the Society's collections at The Athenaeum of Philadelphia; and to Mr. and Mrs. Edward Dart, Samuel J. Dornsife, and Mr. and Mrs. Lewis Seeley for depositing at The Athenaeum important documents in the history of painted finishes that have been used in this book; Robert Skaler, Philadelphia, Pennsylvania; George Talbot, State Historical Society of Wisconsin, Madison, Wisconsin; George B. Tatum, Old Lyme, Connecticut; Beth Twiss-Garrity, the Ebenezer Maxwell Mansion, Philadelphia, Pennsylvania; Richard Tyler, Philadelphia, Pennsylvania; George Vaux, president, The Athenaeum of Philadelphia, for permission to reproduce so many illustrations from the rich holdings of that venerable institution; Donald W. Webb, Lexington, Kentucky; and Frank S. Welsh, Bryn Mawr, Pennsylvania. And last—but certainly not least—special thanks to our patient and persistent editor through two Victorian books in as many years, Channa Taub; and to Keith Kamm, bibliographer, and his assistant, Jean Lenville, who daily for a year have tolerated our demands for ready access to the large collection of often ephemeral paint materials they service at The Athenaeum of Philadelphia. All photographs of historical documents from the collection of the Athenaeum are by Louis Meehan; exterior photographs, unless otherwise noted, are by the authors.

VICTORIAN EXTERIOR DECORATION

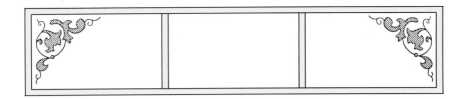

INTRODUCTION

There was a time when an architectural historian or preservationist who proposed painting a Victorian building anything other than white would inevitably be met with an argument. But events of the last decade have changed all that. Tax credits for the rehabilitation of registered buildings, the maturing of the historical preservation movement, and a growing appreciation of Victorian architecture and interior decoration by homeowners seeking value for their housing dollar have helped to spread the word that white is neither historically correct nor any longer the color of choice for most American structures erected in the second half of the nineteenth century.

This ground has been fought over before. Listen to Samuel Sloan, one of America's most influential Victorian architects, in a passage from 1852 that could have been written a century later: "On entering some of our villages, the only color which meets the eye is white. Everything is white; the houses, the fences, the stables, the dog kennels, and sometimes even the trees cannot escape, but get a coat of white wash. . . . Is this taste? Whether it be or not, one thing is certain, that a great change is coming over our people in this respect. They are beginning to see that there are beauties in color as well as form."[1]

The owners, both past and present, of buildings painted white have reason to claim our sympathy: In selecting colors they must make a terrifying decision of the most public nature. Once the choice is made, *everyone* will know. "Many who want to do what will be considered in good taste," wrote Ehrick Kensett Rossiter and Frank Ayers Wright in their 1882 book *Modern House Painting*, "are puzzled to know what colors to use, and how to direct their painter so as to give him a tolerably clear idea of what they want." If the Victorians were uncertain how to paint their houses, can we blame modern owners for repainting year after year in safe, clean white? This choice requires no imagination, no originality, no spark of adventure, no sensitivity to the intent of the original builders—in short, no risk.[2]

This book is designed to reduce the risk and pain of selecting and applying finishes to your Victorian building. The first chapter helps you decide how authentic you want your paint scheme to be. The second chapter then discusses the history of color use and some special finishing techniques used by the Victorians as a regular part of exterior decoration. This will help you understand why some colors are more appropriate than others for buildings of a particular age and style. The third chapter takes you step by step through the process of selecting actual colors for your building. As you will see, it is easier than you may think. We've also matched thirty-four of the most common Victorian colors to the paint lines of four major paint companies: Sherwin-Williams, Benjamin Moore, Glidden, and Devoe. Since we

PLATE 1. *The Queen Victoria Inn at Cape May, New Jersey, as repainted in the historical blue greens of the 1880s, appropriate for a Second Empire–style structure.*

1

PLATE 2. *A Second Empire–style, mansard-roofed house—called a "turreted French-roof villa"—painted in three colors. The window sash color is a rich Indian Red, which is typical for the period, but in addition the sash color has been used to highlight the trim. In spite of this use of red for an accent color, the most important effects are achieved by reversing the body color—Straw or Fawn—and the main trim color—Dark Brownstone. Seeley Bros. Paint Company (New York, 1886).* Collection of Mr. and Mrs. Lewis Seeley, The Athenaeum of Philadelphia

PLATE 3. *The placement of trim colors is particularly important on this Stick-style, vertical-board-sided house of the 1870s in Bridgeton, New Jersey.*

have no affiliation with any of these companies, we don't care which one you use—they are all good, and there are many regional firms that can probably match the colors we discuss. The point is, no matter where you live in America you will be able to paint your Victorian building in a historically accurate way without going to the expense and bother of having special colors mixed.

After you've selected your color(s), we'll help you, in the fourth chapter, to place those colors on your building. We've worked with hundreds of owners like you in all parts of America, and we have a good idea of the kinds of questions you would ask if we were standing with you at this moment in front of your building. What about the roof treatment? Should the shutters be more than one color? Can the porch brackets be picked out to highlight details? You would probably also ask about surface preparation, and in the appendix we discuss common types of paint surface conditions and problems and recommend appropriate treatments so that your carefully thought-out paint scheme will enhance the value of your building, be a source of pride to you, and become a joy to your neighbors.

HOW AUTHENTIC MUST MY PAINT SCHEME BE?

Before launching into the reasons that some colors are more appropriate for the age and style of your Victorian building than others, we would like you to think about what level of *authenticity* you will want to follow. To help you make that decision, we have divided paint schemes into three types: *Scientific*, *Historical*, and *Boutique* or "painted lady"—terms we'll use throughout the pages that follow. This chapter discusses the characteristics of these schemes and outlines what is required for each and some of the problems you may encounter.

SCIENTIFIC

By *Scientific*, we mean the modern standards followed by museums and local landmark buildings, which require that in restoring a building to a specific time in the past, the historical finishes contemporaneous with the restoration target date be scientifically determined. Scientific restoration allows little flexibility in the selection or placement of colors, and requires the services of an architectural-finishes specialist who examines surface finishes under laboratory conditions using a variety of microscopic and chemical techniques. The specialist de-

PLATE 4. *Scientific studies of historical finishes determined the original trim colors for repainting the Maxwell Mansion, an 1859 museum house built of stone in the Norman Gothic style in the Germantown section of Philadelphia.*

termines the number and sequence of paint layers, their color and distribution, and whether any decorative treatments are present (stenciling, marbleizing, graining, sanding); the composition of the paint, and whether it was flat, glossy, or textured; and the probable date of each layer.[1]

Once the physical examination is completed, the historical-paint consultant submits a detailed report—including color notations and samples—usually keyed to the Munsell System of Color Notation (a system developed by Albert H. Munsell early in the twentieth century to provide a systematic means of describing and identifying color). The Munsell notations give you a color guide that is far more reliable than a commercial brand name, which can change over time or even disappear at the whim of the company. And when your structure needs repainting, five to ten years after your restoration, you can return to the Munsell color standard notation and need not attempt to choose new paint based on finishes that have become weathered and faded.

Unfortunately, there are only a few scientifically trained, full-time, historical-architectural-finish consultants in the United States. Their services can be relatively expensive, and may include travel and lodging expenses as well as laboratory and report-drafting time. Also, be warned: Not everyone with a microscope is qualified to determine historical finishes. Even some architectural firms claiming to offer this service to their clients may lack a truly qualified person to take samples or interpret them. Too often the task is assigned to a student intern or the most junior member of the firm, whose knowledge of historical finishes is more hopeful than real. Always ask for the credentials of the person who will actually conduct the investigation, and request copies of some previous reports prepared by that person. If you are still in doubt, check with your State Historic Preservation Officer, the National Trust for Historic Preservation, or a Regional Office of the National Park Service; the staffs of these agencies can provide you with the names and addresses of qualified, independent consultants.

Why can't you prepare your own paint chronology by carefully scraping away each layer of finish and comparing what is revealed to modern paint chips? Because paint is not a stable material. Exposed to radical changes in weather—bleached by the sun, darkened with age—colors simply do not remain the same. The materials themselves may change. For example, linseed oil may yellow, especially when covered for decades by later finishes, and some historic pigments are so fugitive—especially those used to achieve blue and green—that they may alter dramatically over time. To overcome these changes the specialist may expose samples to ultraviolet light—to counteract the yellowing of linseed oil, for example—or subject them to chemical tests, to

Conducting Your Own Investigation of Historical Colors and Finishes

While it is difficult without the help of a trained specialist to obtain a color match that will meet scientific standards of authenticity, you can conduct an investigation that will tell you much about the historical finishes of your building. You can check color placement and learn, for example, whether or not the sash was a different color from the window frames; you can determine whether a molding, a window, or an entire porch is original to the building, and you can uncover layers of paint that will help you *approximate* the colors and finishing techniques used in the past.

Geological terminology is often used by architectural-finish specialists because finishes accumulate in layers—one for each application—that are usually separated from each other by microscopic layers of

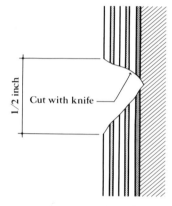

PLATE 13. *A section of paint stratification revealed with a knife.* Drawing by Richard A. Votta

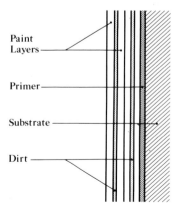

PLATE 12. *Paint stratification.* Drawing by Richard A. Votta

dirt that became embedded in the surface while it was exposed to the elements. This accumulated *stratification* becomes the finish history of your building—its chromochronology (see Plate 12).

The tools you will need to conduct your own investigation are an X-acto knife, an illuminated magnifier (or a magnifying glass and a portable light), some 220-grit wet/dry sandpaper, and lubricating oil. After locating an area of the surface that has been most protected from weathering, cut through all the layers with the knife as shown in Plate 13. This cut need not be larger than ½ inch to 1 inch across, and if you angle the knife blade you will create a slightly dished edge that will expose all the surviving layers down to the substrate.

Now wet the exposed area liberally with lubricating oil and with a circular motion sand the layers smooth to create a dish that will gradually come to look like tree rings that may be "read" outward from the center of exposed wood (or plaster,

Paint layers sanded smooth —

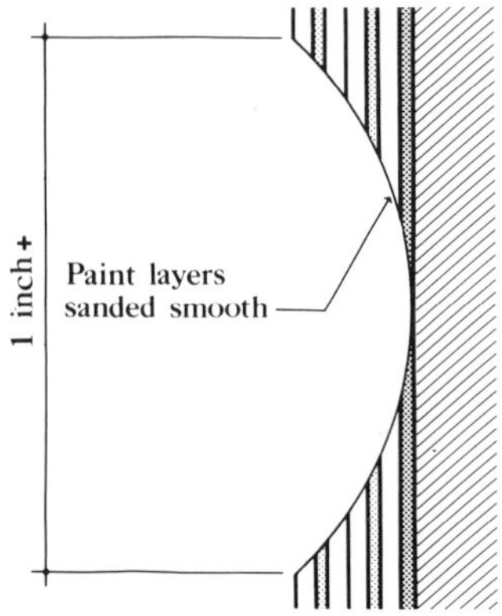

PLATE 14. *Layers of paint stratification that have been sanded.* Drawing by Richard A. Votta

iron, etc.) to the most recent, undisturbed layer. Examine these exposed rings under magnification to identify the first or subsequent color that is to be matched (Plate 14). Using commercial paint remover, you can expose a 2-inch square of the layer to be matched and compare it to commercially available paint samples. National manufacturers such as Sherwin-Williams, Benjamin Moore, Glidden, and Devoe offer up to 1600 colors in their retail lines, and you can usually obtain a fairly close match.

For additional information on conducting your own investigation, read Penelope H. Batcheler, *Paint Color Research and Restoration*, Technical Leaflet 15 (Nashville, Tenn.: American Association for State and Local History, 1968). This four-page leaflet is available for fifty cents from AASLH, 1400 8th Avenue S., Nashville, Tenn. 37203. More technical sources are cited in the Notes section of this book.

PLATE 5. *Although Acorn Hall, c. 1853 in Morristown, New Jersey, was not repainted in its original color (gray), the trustees selected hues appropriate to the third quarter of the nineteenth century—Straw and Reddish Brown.*

determine the original pigment. Furthermore, the specialist understands past painting practices and is less likely to be misled by the discovery of Spanish-brown or yellow-ocher coats next to the surface. Both of these were common primer coats in the nineteenth century—resulting perhaps in an unusually high number of yellow or brown "restored" Victorian paint schemes.[2]

Occasionally a museum house committee or curator will object to the finishes uncovered by the historical-finishes consultant when the findings differ dramatically from contemporary tastes. When this happens, the committee or curator should be scrupulous in executing the findings. The responsibility of a museum house—particularly one being interpreted as the residence of a particular person or family—is to represent taste at the target date, not a modern idealization of that taste. Public restorations have a didactic responsibility to interpret the past by its own lights—and colors. Does this mean that there is no flexibility of color choice? Not necessarily. Let's take a hypothetical example. The building being restored is an Italianate house erected in 1855 and painted gray. In 1878, however, the family added a new wing and repainted the entire house green. Depending on the target date selected for the restoration and interpretation, the curator or committee might restore the gray scheme or the green one, although most authorities would strongly favor the latter as more nearly portraying the complete house as it actually appeared at a given time in the past.

HISTORICAL

Of the three levels of authenticity discussed here, the *Historical* is the one most likely to appeal to private owners who are not planning to live in museums, and to curators of museum houses not being restored to illustrate the residency—and thus the taste in exterior decoration—of a particular person or family. Aside from the greater cost of the Scientific approach in determining historical colors, we also recognize that color choice is a matter of intimate preference. To insist that a private home be painted green simply because it originally was painted that color would be foolish. No matter how historically accurate a color may be, you won't use what you don't like; you will want to express your personal tastes. Nonetheless, most owners of Victorian buildings realize that some colors and methods of application are more appropriate—more sympathetic—than others to the age and style of the building. Fortunately, there is a wide enough range of colors that are historically appropriate to allow you to express your individuality while being fair to the age and style of the building. To achieve a historical paint scheme, you must observe the two principles of Historical-level authenticity:

1. The colors applied to any building should be selected from those that were available and considered appropriate for the date, type, and style of

PLATE 6. *Modest Victorian houses of no particular style are found in historic districts across America. Here the four owners of twin houses cooperated in color selection, assisted by a representative of the local housing office charged with enforcing the color clause in the historic-district zoning ordinance. The house on the left has a Light Drab body, Dark Drab trim, and Reddish Brown sash. The house on the right has a Light Blue Green body with trim in Dark Blue Stone and sash painted in Shutter Green. (The unfortunate color change in the gable of the house on the left resulted from two weekend painters working from two cans of the same brand and color of paint on different weekends. Had a single painter started at the top and worked across the entire gable, such differences, which can occur even when painting with seemingly identical colors, would not have been so obvious.)*

the building at the time of its design and construction.

2. Those colors—whatever they may be—should be applied to the structure to enhance the design in the manner intended by the original designer, builder, and owners.

Once freed of the tyranny of the *specific* taste of the original designer or owner of your building, the whole spectrum of the colorful Victorians becomes available to you. This book will help you select from among the wide variety of historical paint schemes and finishing techniques those that are appropriate for the age, style, and location of your building while taking into account your individual color preferences. In working with hundreds of owners in all parts of the country we have rarely failed to reach agreement on a combination of colors and placement that satisfied both the owners' taste and the historical requirements of the building.

Historical is the level of authenticity most often mandated by local historic-district ordinances and for buildings being rehabilitated under *The Secretary of the Interior's Standards for Historic Preservation Projects with Guidelines for Applying the Standards* for tax-credit certification—although the latter will naturally favor the use of original

colors scientifically determined. The most recent edition (1983) of the *Standards* states that colors should be "appropriate to the historical building and the district."[3]

Many American towns and cities are writing clauses into their historic-district zoning ordinances that require building owners within the designated area to submit their proposed color schemes for approval before beginning to repaint (samples of such clauses are available from the Legal Department, National Trust for Historic Preservation, 1785 Massachusetts Avenue, Washington, D.C. 20036). We have worked with several communities that have developed ordinances requiring historical paint colors, and in our observation the positive benefits—higher property values and sense of neighborhood pride—in all cases far outweighed the minor irritation of determining an "approved" paint scheme.

The skillful use of historically appropriate colors is one of the least expensive and most rapid means for achieving design compatibility within a district. Since most of our towns are less homogenized than Colonial Williamsburg—or the carefully tended historical areas of Charleston, South Carolina, or Hudson, Ohio—there is a need to blend in otherwise discordant structures. The next time you visit a historical neighborhood that appeals to you, look closely at all the buildings on a

PLATE 7. *A streetscape of brick, stone, shingle, and stucco Colonial Revival houses of the type found in many late-nineteenth-century suburban developments. These, rendered in body colors of Buff and Straw and trimmed in Medium Brownstone and Olive, appeared in Harrison Bros. & Co.'s "Town and Country Ready Mixed Paints" (Philadelphia, c. 1884).* Collection of Mr. and Mrs. Edward D. Dart, The Athenaeum of Philadelphia

PLATE 8. *F. W. Devoe & Company cautioned that houses standing near one another should be painted following the rules of harmony by contrast. "The general effect is rich, warm and elegant, the architectural details being brought into agreeable prominence." The house on the left is painted a Medium Brownstone trimmed in Light Brownstone and Dark Olive. The house on the right is painted Straw with trim in Medium Brownstone and Bronze Green. Notice that the turned porch posts of the Queen Anne–style houses are picked out in the body colors of each house.* Exterior Decoration *(New York: F. W. Devoe & Company, 1885), plate XV.* Dornsife Collection of the Victorian Society in America at The Athenaeum of Philadelphia

PLATE 9. *The handsome late Victorian houses of San Francisco's Steiner Street at Alamo Square (shown on this page and opposite) are among the most publicized examples of the Boutique approach to Victorian exterior decoration.*

typical street. We suspect you will be surprised at how many do not conform in age or style with the overall impression you have of the neighborhood. Similar scale and compatible colors are the secrets of the most appealing historic districts all across America.

BOUTIQUE

The third approach to the exterior decoration of Victorian buildings is the *Boutique*, or California "painted lady," style, which at first glance bears little resemblance to nineteenth-century practice. According to an article on California in a paint trade journal, "An epidemic of striped houses has struck the interior towns of the State. They who would be in fashion, says the San Francisco *Examiner*, must dress their dwellings in gaudy coats of brown and yellow, cream and maroon, gray, yellow, pink, red, or olive, joined with some hue in violent contrast. The body of the house is usually painted with one color, the cornice, corner boards, window and door frames being in savage contrast. Occasionally this bizarre effect is carried still further, and some very costly villas have tried a different color on each story, while the fancy shingled roofs are painted all colors of the rainbow. This chromatic craze has reached the city, and some really tasteful houses are marred by this extraordinary style of exterior decoration." The article continues to remark

that this California taste is "illogical and fallacious" and a violation of "good morals"; the "steady observance" of some color combinations, readers are warned, "may excite madness. . . ." Contrary to what might be thought, this condemnation of northern California paint practices is not in reaction to some modern "painted lady" on the shores of the San Francisco Bay; rather, it appeared in *Painting and Decorating* magazine in December 1892.[4]

The modern Boutique approach has its roots partly in the traditional California preference for more complex paint schemes and in the colorist movement that began in San Francisco in the 1960s as an act of self-expression. As these colorful creations began to gain attention, architectural preservationists realized their media potential. A highly visible structure is harder to pull down than one no one notices, and branding these often garish structures "painted ladies" was an inspired piece of public relations. Only the Golden Gate Bridge and the famous cable cars surpass these houses as San Francisco tourist symbols.

In both color and placement, the twentieth-century Boutique approach to exterior decoration differs from historical practice. The colors tend toward pure chroma or brilliant pastels and are lavishly applied, often in xylophonic bars of graduated color that dance over the spectrum. At their best the Boutique painters' creations can turn ordinary buildings into delightful street art; in the hands of less skilled practitioners, the results can be disastrous for the building and the neighborhood. Paint, in addition to providing protection from the elements,

PLATE 10. *Particularly characteristic of some Boutique painters' work is the use of white for trim against a darker body, as shown here on the former Imperial Russian consulate (1875) in San Francisco, now operated as a bed-and-breakfast inn.*

is a cosmetic. As any cosmetologist will confirm, the line between highlighting the best features and creating a tart is easily crossed. In 1914 a paint company warned, "Good lines, right proportions, proper arrangement—all may be destroyed by freak painting in wrong colors. . . . Every neighborhood has some illustration of an otherwise excellent house made hideous by somebody's blunders in wrong colors or too many or bad combinations of body and trimming colors." Even the official architectural journal of California grumbled in 1885, "We have from time to time called attention to the crazy style of architecture adopted by a few of our younger would-be architects. One of the principal ingredients of this style is to cover the buildings, when finished, with a bountiful supply of paint, using more colors by far than the tailor who designed Joseph's Coat. . . . Red, yellow, chocolate, orange, everything that is loud is in fashion, and the entire exterior is so gay that a Virginia creeper or a wisteria would be bold, indeed, if it dare set leaf or tendril there."[5]

Ironically, modern homeowners in San Francisco who adopted the "painted lady" approach in the late 1960s and 1970s have learned a painful and often expensive lesson. Boutique color schemes do not age well; colors of widely different value tend to fade at different rates, especially when exposed to strong sunlight, and it often has become a race to see whether the owner tires first of a house perpetually in party dress or of the cost of annual maintenance. San Francisco has recently witnessed a trend toward more historical uses of color—particularly the return to a single body color picked out with a lighter tint or darker shade of the principal color and dark sash—a tradition well documented by local architectural historians.

Thus, you must carefully consider whether the Boutique approach is indeed appropriate for your building. Colors that work for Disneyland or a beach-front cottage can rarely be introduced successfully into the typical American Victorian neighborhood, especially as the trim for a masonry building. A homeowner on holiday in San Francisco, Cape May, or Key West—where the infection has been most rampant—should not return home with the mistaken belief that such colors and placement are appropriate for all Victorian buildings wherever they may be. Our warning is that these "painted ladies" are best not transported across state lines.

PLATE 11. *Widely different values between body and trim colors as on 2022 California Street (c. 1885) in San Francisco* (left and right above) *are now less common. The house on the left, for example, 908 Steiner Street (c. 1899) in San Francisco, which in the 1960s was known as the "psychedelic house" because of its bizarre paint scheme, has recently been repainted gray and white; such treatments are more typical of current practice (see also Plates 88, top, and 111, top).*

COLORFUL VICTORIANS, 1840-1900

Before sitting down with several dozen color cards in an effort to come up with a historical paint scheme, you need to determine the age and style of your building. Aside from the satisfaction to be derived from saying, "It's a late Queen Anne built about 1890" or "We live in an Italianate villa of 1856," the date and style of your building are the keys that will help you unlock the secrets of how its exterior was originally decorated. Tastes in architectural style and decoration changed dramatically in the second half of the nineteenth century, chiefly in response to sweeping social and technological developments. In particular, the colors used to decorate American buildings in the post–Civil War decades were influenced by a number of technological innovations. If your house was erected after about 1870, for example, it probably was painted with ready-mixed paint. At that time the paint industry developed machinery to grind pigment in white lead and oil, and containers in which the ready-mixed product could be safely shipped. However, if your building is in a part of the country that the railroads didn't reach until fairly late in the nineteenth century, it is unlikely that the owners used the richer and more colorful ready-mixed paints. It was only as the railroad network spanned the nation that large paint manufacturers in urban centers such as New York, Philadelphia, and Chicago were able to reach distant markets.[1]

As the growing transportation network made the nation more accessible after the Civil War, paint manufacturers took advantage of technological advances in printing—the development of inexpensive wood-pulp paper and high-speed, steam-driven presses—to have printed and distributed colorful advertising brochures and architectural pattern books that reached thousands of Americans building residential, commercial, and institutional structures. The paint manufacturers were pursuing a growing market. The population of the United States doubled nearly twice over between 1840 and 1890—17 million to 63 million people—which led in turn to dramatic growth in the building trades and in hundreds of companies created to supply their needs.[2]

The chances are that your building is not an architect's original design but the product of architectural pattern books—such as E. C. Hussey's *Home Building . . . from New York to San Francisco* (New York, 1876)—widely used by local contractors and of trade catalogues that supplied such diverse products as stoves, tile, millwork, and paint. Both helped to homogenize American building in the last decades of the nineteenth century. By the late 1880s, houses built in Central City, Colorado, and in Zanesville, Ohio, shared stylistic characteristics as well as the same palette of colors, many of which were much darker and richer than those advocated by the pre–Civil War generation of architects.

PLATE 15. *The variety of textures, irregularity of plan, the exposed structural members, and small panes of glass in the upper sash—all characteristics of the Queen Anne style—call attention to the need for careful outlining and color changes as clearly shown in this flank elevation. Three body colors—Medium Brownstone, Terra Cotta, and Amber—a trim painted in Old Gold, and sash in Shutter Green complete this example from* The Painter *(March 1885).* The Athenaeum of Philadelphia Collection

What Style Is My House?

Over the years we have been asked to suggest a single-volume guide to American architecture written for the layman, something that would help develop a basic vocabulary of terms and styles. As yet we haven't found a *single* book that is entirely satisfactory, but J.-B. Blumenson's *Identifying American Architecture, 1600–1945* (Nashville, Tenn.: American Association for State and Local History, 1977) comes as close as any now on the market. Blumenson's purpose is "to provide photographic illustrations of buildings, architectural details, elements, and forms to enable the user to make visual associations and to begin to recognize styles and elements." If you cannot differentiate among Second Empire, Stick-style, Eastlake, and Shingle-style houses, or if you refer to a trefoil as a "whatchamacallit" or a console as a

"thingamajig," this inexpensive, compact paperback (118 pages, 214 photographs) is the book for you. Less detailed than Blumenson's work, but nonetheless useful, is John Poppeliers's 46-page pamphlet *What Style Is It?*, published in 1977 by the National Trust for Historic Preservation.

Once you have mastered the basics of style and terminology, there are several introductory books that are more detailed and textual. Our favorite is Marcus Whiffen's *American Architecture Since 1780: A Guide to the Styles* (Cambridge, Mass.: MIT Press, 1969). If you wish to cross the threshold—literally and figuratively—and get into considerations of both floor plans and building theory, you will want to look at Leland M. Roth's *A Concise History of American Architecture* (New York: Harper & Row, 1979) and David P. Handlin, *The American Home* (Boston: Little, Brown, 1979). You may find *The American Home* to be particularly interesting because it

focuses on domestic building and contains chapters on the developing technology of heating, bathrooms, and kitchens.

For an even more detailed look at the residential Victorian building, check the specialized works listed in the bibliographies of the books mentioned above. The most important scholarly study is still Vincent J. Scully, Jr., *The Shingle Style and the Stick Style* (New Haven: Yale University Press, 1971), which may be heavy going for a general reader. In a much more popular vein, however, are two books by John Maass: *The Gingerbread Age* (New York: Rinehart, 1957; Greenwich House, 1983) and *The Victorian Home in America* (New York: Hawthorn Books, 1972), both of which have lively texts and hundreds of photographs that celebrate domestic building from the second half of the last century. Both are now out of print but regularly appear on discount remainder lists and can be obtained at most large libraries.

Roughly speaking, there were four major color phases in the nineteenth century: late Federal and Neoclassical (to c. 1840); Gothic and Italianate Revival, or early Victorian (c. 1840–1870); high Victorian (c. 1870–1890); and Colonial Revival (c. 1890–1920), which saw a renewed interest in Neoclassical detailing and in early American architecture. All four periods have fairly definable color palettes, ranging from the dominant white of late Federal through the pale earth tones of early Victorian and the dark, rich—if somewhat "muddy"— colors that most people associate with high Victorian buildings to a gradual return to white and light pastels during the Colonial Revival. This is unquestionably an oversimplification. For example, late Victorian structures in the Shingle style and bungalows heavily influenced by the Arts and Crafts Movement (see Plates 39c and 108) continued to utilize the rich, colorful palette of deep reds, browns, and greens even as the Colonial Revival architects were specifying white houses with green shutters, or blue, gray, or yellow bodies trimmed with white (see Plates 35 and 36). Therefore, if you want to select historically appropriate colors, it is essential that you determine your building's age, as well as the major stylistic influences that shaped it.[3] (See "What Style Is My House?" above and watch for stylistic references in the plate captions.)

But we're getting ahead of the story. Let's go back to the early nineteenth century and review how American

PLATE 16.

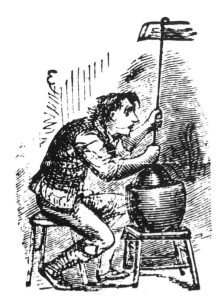

PLATE 17.

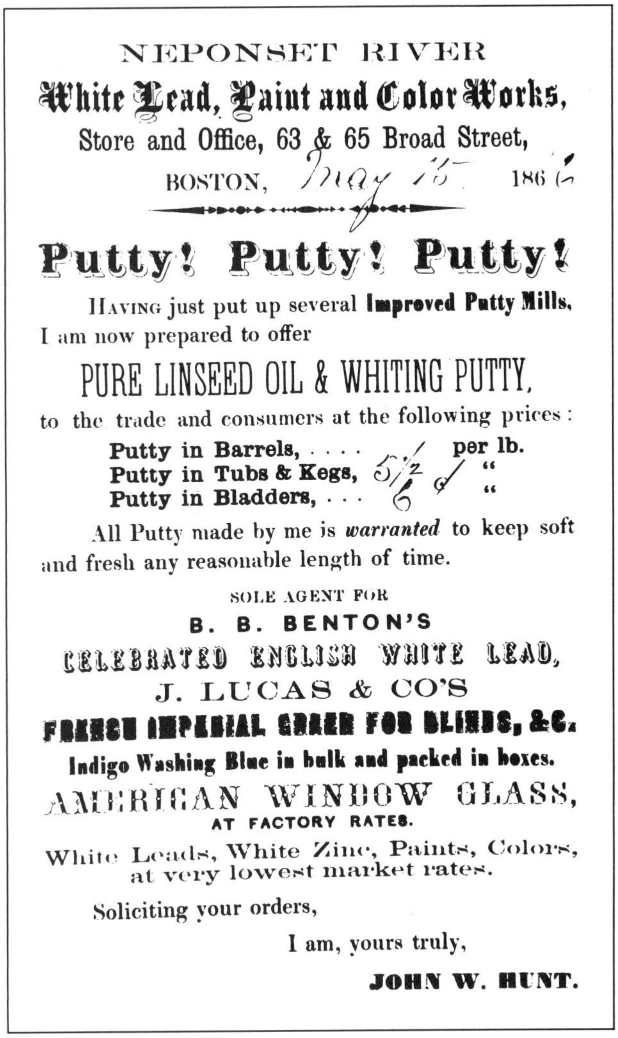

tastes in color changed over a century and how the development of ready-mixed paint altered the way housepainters work.

The arrival of housepainters can be something of an event. The unloading of ladders and drop cloths richly encrusted with dribbles and splotches from previous jobs, the laying out of carefully tended brushes, the opening of shiny cans of smooth oil paint, linseed oil, and pungent turpentine—all are guaranteed to draw a crowd of neighborhood children. With minor variations, painters have worked this way for a century; yet the process of *preparing* to paint a house today differs greatly from what was required of the early-nineteenth-century painter. According to Hezekiah Reynolds, a New England painter who published *Directions for House and Ship Painting* in 1812, the painter first had to clarify his linseed oil by boiling it in a brass or copper pot with red lead. Then, to prepare the paints for outside work, the worker would: "Take a smooth iron kettle of middling size, and an iron ball weighing from 12 to 24 pounds; and suspend them in some convenient place, by a rope or chain; put into the kettle from four to six pounds of paint dry, and grind it until thoroughly pulverized. . . . After a sufficient quantity of paint is ground dry . . . put into the same kettle six or eight pounds of the dry paint at each time; and add oil until the ball will move easy and free—add also the materials necessary to produce the color which you propose to paint . . . ; mix them thoroughly with the ball, and place the paint in suitable vessels for use." According to Reynolds, the normal exterior colors mixed in this fashion were white, cream (an off-white), straw (a pale yellow), and orange; pea, parrot, and grass greens; red, slate (a blue gray), and black; he implies, however, that interior colors could be mixed for exterior use.[4]

Notwithstanding the range of exterior colors mentioned by Reynolds and the occasional discovery of such colors in the scientific examination of surviving structures erected in the early nineteenth century, the remarks of Victorian architects and critics strongly suggest that Americans overwhelmingly favored white for their residential and public buildings. And given what we know of early paint-mixing techniques, white was certainly the easiest color for the painter to mix to avoid variations between batches.

According to Andrew Jackson Downing, whose views on virtually every topic relating to horticulture and architecture were widely followed in the mid-nineteenth century,

NEPONSET RIVER

White Lead, Paint and Color Works,

Store and Office, 63 & 65 Broad Street,

BOSTON, 186

Putty! Putty! Putty!

HAVING just put up several **Improved Putty Mills**, I am now prepared to offer

PURE LINSEED OIL & WHITING PUTTY,

to the trade and consumers at the following prices:

Putty in Barrels, ... **per lb.**
Putty in Tubs & Kegs, "
Putty in Bladders, . . . "

All Putty made by me is *warranted* to keep soft and fresh any reasonable length of time.

SOLE AGENT FOR

B. B. BENTON'S

CELEBRATED ENGLISH WHITE LEAD,

J. LUCAS & CO'S

FRENCH IMPERIAL GREEN FOR BLINDS, &C.

Indigo Washing Blue in bulk and packed in boxes.

AMERICAN WINDOW GLASS,

AT FACTORY RATES.

White Leads, White Zinc, Paints, Colors, at very lowest market rates.

Soliciting your orders,

I am, yours truly,

JOHN W. HUNT.

PLATE 18. *A typical advertising broadside published on the eve of the ready-mixed-paint revolution. Notice the mention of "French Imperial Green for Blinds, &c."* The Athenaeum of Philadelphia Collection

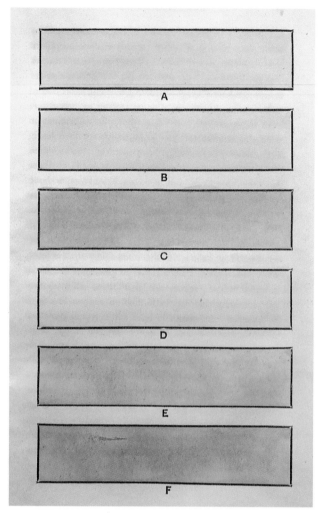

There is one colour . . . frequently employed by house painters, which we feel bound to protest against most heartily, as entirely unsuitable, and in bad taste. This is *white*, which is so universally applied to our wooden houses of every size and description. The glaring nature of this colour, when seen in contrast with the soft green foliage, renders it extremely unpleasant to an eye attuned to harmony of coloring, and nothing but its very great prevalence in the United States could render even men of some taste so heedless of its bad effect.[5]

Not content to publish a hand-tinted plate of alternative colors (Plate 19), Downing continued his attack in the *Horticulturist* magazine and in his influential book *The Architecture of Country Houses*. The exterior color of a house, he argued in the latter, "is of more importance than is usually supposed, since, next to the form itself, the colour is the first impression which the eye receives in approaching it—and, in some cases, the colour makes its impression, even before we fully comprehend the form of the building."[6] Downing and other American architects and critics who favored the picturesque thought buildings should be integrated with nature, not imposed upon it. No less a figure than James Fenimore Cooper, author of the popular Leather-Stocking Tales, objected to the glaring purity and rationality of Neoclassicism that starkly declared Americans' separation from the environment. The critics felt that natural coloring, picturesque lines, and landscaping that

PLATE 19. *One of the first efforts to provide actual colors in a book on architecture was Andrew Jackson Downing's hand-colored plate in* Cottage Residences *(New York, 1842). "As it is difficult to convey in words a proper idea of delicate shades of colour," he wrote, "and as we think the subject one of very great importance in domestic architecture, we have given specimens . . . of six shades of colour highly suitable for the exterior of cottages and villas. A, B, and C, are shades of gray, and D, E, F, of drab or fawn colour; which will be found pleasing and harmonious in any situation in the country. Stuccoed or cemented buildings should be marked off in courses, and tinted to resemble some mellow stone; Bath, Portland stone, or any other of the light free-stone shades, are generally most agreeable." Dornsife Collection of the Victorian Society in America at The Athenaeum of Philadelphia*

PLATE 20. *Masonry worker scoring stucco to simulate dressed stone blocks (ashlar) at The Athenaeum of Philadelphia. The pattern follows Downing's suggestion and reproduces original scoring specified in 1847 by the building's architect, John Notman. The color is Medium Brownstone.*

PLATE 21. *One of the English sources mentioned by Andrew Jackson Downing was Robert Lugar's* Villa Architecture *(London, 1828), which contains this picturesque Gothic-style house similar to those published in Downing's books. The body is a Buff color and the trim Light Brownstone.* Dornsife Collection of the Victorian Society in America at The Athenaeum of Philadelphia

softened the harshness of masonry and sawed boards helped to restore the balance between man and his surroundings. According to the architect Calvert Vaux, a white Neoclassical house "is distinctly protruded from the surrounding scenery, and instead of grouping and harmonizing with it, asserts a right to carry on a separate business of its own account; and this lack of sympathy between the building and its surroundings is very disagreeable to an artistic eye. . . ." Calling for designs "adapted to the location, and not the location to the design," Vaux favored a picturesque blending of the house and the natural landscape; "every attempt to force individual buildings into prominent notice is an evidence either of a vulgar desire for notoriety at any sacrifice, or of an ill-educated eye and taste."[7]

Downing suggested that houses be painted in colors found in nature to harmonize with their surroundings. "Much of the beauty of landscapes depends on what painters call *breadth of tone*—which is caused by broad masses of colours that harmonize and blend agreeably together. . . . ," he explained in *The Architecture of Country Houses*. Downing advised homeowners that "In buildings, we should copy those that [nature] offers chiefly to the eye—such as those of the soil, rocks, wood, and the bark of trees—the materials of which houses are

built. These materials offer us the best and most natural study from which harmonious colours for the houses themselves should be taken." (Not green, however, because "houses are not built of grass or leaves." On this point, many of Downing's followers differed with the master and soon suggested green as an appropriate color for the body of houses.) Buildings should be painted "*soft and quiet shades* called neutral tints, such as fawn, drab, grey, brown, etc., and . . . all positive colours, such as white, yellow, red, blue, black, etc., should always be avoided. . . ." In addition, the size and placement of a house should influence its color. *"In proportion as a house is exposed to view, let its hue be darker, and where it is much concealed by foliage, a very light shade of colour is to be preferred."* If a house is large, it "may very properly receive a somewhat sober hue, expressive of dignity," but if the structure is a small cottage, it should be painted a lighter color, "a cheerful and lively tint."[8]

Drawing on English authors such as Robert Lugar (Plate 21) and Francis Goodwin whose books on architecture he recommended, Downing favored first the "hue of English freestone, called *Portland stone—a quiet fawn* colour" achieved by blending white, yellow ocher, and Spanish brown, which yields a light, warm gold. "Next to this," he states, "we like a *warm gray*, that is, a gray mixed with a very little red, and some yellow. . . ." As will be discussed in Chapter 4, Downing explains at some length the necessity of picking out certain details of the trim—window facings, shutters, cornices, porches—in another color. "The simplest practical rule that we can suggest for effecting this, in the most satisfactory and agreeable manner, is the following: Choose paint of some neutral tint that is quite satisfactory, and, if the tint is a *light* one, let the facings of the windows, cornices, etc., be painted several *shades* darker, of the same colour. The blinds may either be a still darker shade than the facings, or else the darkest green." C. W. Elliot, who generally followed Downing, argued in 1848 that exterior trim "should be a little darker than the body of the house, instead of lighter, as is now so common."[9]

During the decade prior to the Civil War, a number of other architectural critics restated Downing's views, most notably Henry W. Cleaveland, William and Samuel Backus, Gervase Wheeler, M. Field, and Calvert Vaux. Until more detailed studies of surviving buildings from the 1845–1870 period are conducted, we may only speculate on the extent to which the new coloration was adopted. Architect-designed buildings from the late 1840s through the Civil War, especially in the Gothic and Italianate Revival styles, probably reflected the new taste. Vernacular and traditional buildings in more or less Neoclassical revival styles probably tended to follow the white-with-green-shutters color scheme. In the essay "Art in House Painting," a writer for F. W. Devoe & Company in the 1880s summarized the evolution of color choice in this way:

The change came very gradually, the white being at first tempered for the sake of variety with cold tints of grey, lavender, green, blue, and other colors, totally unfit for the purpose they were intended to serve, but still of value as stepping-stones to better things; the rare examples of the use of deeper shades, of warm rich tints and a variety of colors in exterior decoration, were falsely spoken of as "loud," when really, compared with the old style of painting, their effect was subdued and restful. The new idea in painting, as it was termed, had, however, found friends, it was permanently before the world, and gradually the sole consideration of utility became tempered with a desire for artistic effect.[10]

Certainly by 1861, when John Riddell published the first American architectural pattern book with full-color plates of residential buildings, the Downing colors were much in evidence (see Plates 23 and 52). The palette Riddell illustrates is still somewhat lighter than that offered by the late 1860s "Homestead Colors" sample card of F. W. Devoe & Company reproduced in Plate 24. This card is one of the earliest examples of American ready-mixed paint samples, and it is one of the few containing only the low-saturated, muted colors associated with Downing and the other architects of the picturesque.[11]

The shifting fashion in color did cause comment. In *House-painting: Plain and Decorative*, published in 1868, John W. Masury cautioned, "We must now guard against the . . . extreme, and not suffer our houses to be streaked

PLATE 22. *The architect Joseph C. Wells designed the H. C. Bowen residence, Woodstock, Connecticut, in the Gothic Revival style c. 1845.*

PLATE 23. *This Gothic cottage costing $5,000 to build on the eve of the Civil War relies on its ornamental bargeboard (cut from two-inch-thick white pine), a striped porch roof and floor (not visible here), and green scalloped flashing (joining metal roof to side wall) for effect. Downing would probably have approved of the pale Buff or Straw-colored stucco, although he might have recommended a trim color darker than the body. John Riddell,* Architectural Designs for Model Country Residences *(1861).* The Athenaeum of Philadelphia Collection

PLATE 24. *Issued in the late 1860s, this paint card of "Homestead Colors" by F. W. Devoe & Company soon would be a ubiquitous form of advertising. These paint samples originally were coated with a clear oil-resin varnish for protection which had yellowed with age and was removed before this photograph was taken.* The Athenaeum of Philadelphia Collection

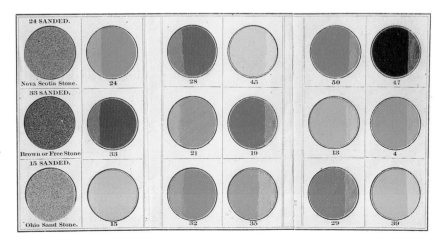

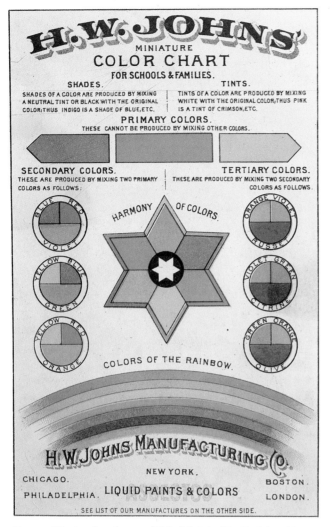

PLATE 25. *A color chart published by the H. W. Johns Manufacturing Company in 1890 to teach primary, secondary, and tertiary colors.* The Athenaeum of Philadelphia Collection

PLATE 26.

with colors and tints laid on by unskillful hands, without regard to harmony or tasteful arrangement. The fashion for compound hues, neutral tints, grays, and other so-called quiet colors, is giving place to a preference for combinations of red, blue, yellow, and other colors of the prism. It has been the custom to decry these colors as gaudy. It is only when they are put together without due regard to their suitableness to each other, and their relative quantities in the arrangement they require, that they appear gaudy and glaring."[12]

As the use of color became more complex in the post–Civil War years, architects and paint manufacturers began to specify rules based less on personal judgment and more on the growing body of color theory. Most writers relied upon the work of David Ramsay Hay of Edinburgh, Scotland, a housepainter and author of *The Laws of Harmonious Colouring*, published in 1828. Nearly every article on the subject of color during the 1850s and 1860s referred to Hay's work, including the most popular magazine for women, *Godey's Lady's Book*, and Hay's theories were well known to many American householders. Masury included Hay's theories and described two approaches to color harmony. The first was "harmony by analogy," that is, using those colors next to one another on the color wheel. Masury's examples included crimson and purple, yellow and gold, crimson and rich brown. The second was "harmony by contrast," employing those colors opposite one another on the color wheel (complementary colors), such as scarlet and blue, orange and blue, yellow and black, white and black.[13]

Sophisticated studies into the effects of *adjacent colors* on one another also influenced the palette used for exterior decoration. The most significant of these was the work of Michel Eugène Chevreul (1786–1889), long-lived Director of Dyes for the Gobelins tapestry works. His text on colors was published originally in France in 1839, and followed by an English translation, *The Principles of Harmony and Contrast of Colours and Their Application to the Arts*, in 1854. Chevreul's principles appeared in America in *The Painter, Gilder, and Varnisher's Companion*, which ran to sixteen editions between 1869 and 1873. The magazine *House Painting and Decorating* considered Chevreul's work so important it urged readers to consult the English translation because "It is an error, of course, to suppose that the art of arranging colors so as to produce the best effects in painting is entirely dependent on the taste of the operator; for harmony of coloring is determined by fixed natural laws." The magazine's editors stressed that fashion required more knowledge by the trade because "the increased demand for fine decorative or ornamental work renders it of considerable importance to the painter to make himself acquainted with these laws; as without some attention to them, the most elaborate and elegant designs of the architect, and the finest colors that can

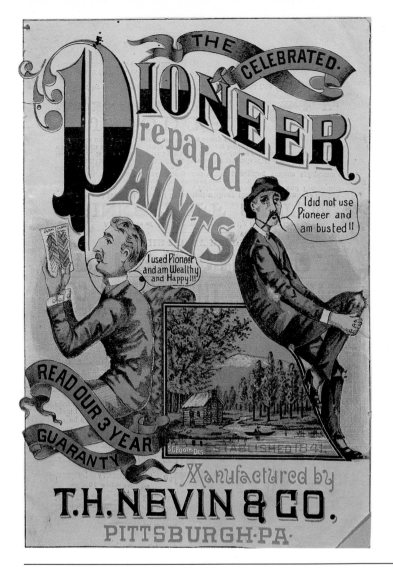

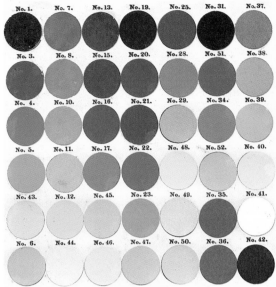

PLATE 28. *The wide range of colors used for exterior decoration in the late 1860s and early 1870s is well illustrated in this rare Harrison Bros. & Co.'s "Town and Country Ready Prepared Paints" paint card of 1871. The pale Downing colors survive together with the darker tertiary palette that will dominate the next twenty years.* Collection of Frank Welsh

PLATE 27. *Anticipating Madison Avenue copywriters of the twentieth century, Victorians blatantly suggested that the key to happiness and wealth was the use of one product over another. The prosperous gent on the left is contemplating a sample card from Pioneer Prepared Paints. T. H. Nevin & Company,* Annual Almanac *(Pittsburgh, 1886).* The Athenaeum of Philadelphia Collection

be produced, may yield but an indifferent, if not decidedly unpleasing result."[14]

From his work with tapestry dyes, Chevreul observed that certain colors placed adjacent to some hues appear to shift in hue or value while the same colors adjacent to other hues might intensify. Chevreul was not the first to witness these phenomena, but he was the first to record them systematically. For instance, he discovered that complementary colors adjacent to one another in patterns appear more intense because the retina of the eye produces an "afterimage" of the complement of each color. For example, the afterimage caused by looking at red is green, and of green, red—in both cases the complements. The human eye has this response to all colors; thus yellow will cause a purple afterimage and orange will cause blue. Because of the afterimage, two colors adjacent to one another but *not* complements will appear altered in hue. Chevreul's studies showed that red next to orange appears as a purplish red next to a yellowish orange. Furthermore, he discovered that white, black, and gray also affect the hues adjacent to them, making

them appear deeper, lighter, and richer respectively. Chevreul's findings regarding color relationships greatly influenced critics and through them the decoration of buildings in the 1870s and 1880s.[15]

The use of the richer colors was also encouraged by the American paint companies who wanted to create a market for their ready-mixed products. The Wadsworth, Martinez & Longman Company stated in the 1880s, "The extensive distribution of Color Cards, Lithographs of Buildings in color, and many other methods placed before the public, to aid in making suitable selection of proper shades of color for painting, has provided the means to change from simple white with green blinds to the many pleasing shades of color now presented upon almost every residence." An article in the November 1885 issue of *House Painting and Decorating* magazine, entitled "What the Art of House Painting Owes to the Manufacturers of Ready-Mixed Paints," explained that "as soon as ready-mixed paints, or paints ready for use, began to be introduced a field of new and rich design was opened to the painter and owners of property, which

circumstances had previously barred. Shades and tints of color were prepared, which had hitherto been beyond the painter's reach." The publication of sample cards "enabled tints and shades of color to be *seen* and their effect in combination determined." The writer concluded, "the ladies of a household are now enabled to exercise their proverbial taste, and have a voice in the selection of colors for the beautifying of their dwellings." Ready-mixed paints produced controlled colors in a variety of values from light to dark and enabled homeowners to choose from *tertiary colors* (those formed by mixing two secondary colors; see Plate 25 chart) such as citrine, olive, and russet to create the complex paint schemes based on Chevreul's laws of color harmony. Although the distinctions may appear to us to be distressingly complicated, writers of the period generally grasped and followed them. Furthermore, an understanding of nineteenth-century rules of color harmony renders color use during the last quarter of the nineteenth century intelligible and its use in restoration less arbitrary.[16]

America did not automatically switch to the rich colors

of the post–Civil War years with the arrival of the first train loaded with Lucas, Devoe, Seeley Brothers, or Sherwin-Williams ready-mixed paints. The coloring of America was a gradual process—and one that did not endure much beyond the turn of the century. The introduction of richer, deeper colors in the 1870s is reflected in Harrison Bros. & Co.'s "Town and Country" paint sample card of 1871 (see Plate 28). The lighter colors recommended by Downing survive (as they will throughout the century), but more greens, oranges, and olives have begun to creep into the palette. Two movements encouraged this change. First, the growing complexity of architecture as America moved from the Gothic, Italianate, and Second Empire revivals toward Queen Anne, Stick-, Eastlake, and Shingle-style buildings. Second, there was a shift, encouraged by the Arts and Crafts Movement, toward an emphasis on materials, texture, massing, and exposed structure—which required richer colors of aged wood, weathered shingles, mossy stone, and sun-bleached terra cotta. Isaac H. Hobbs wrote in the second edition of *Hobbs' Architecture* (1876), "Designing a building is like a battle upon canvas of color,

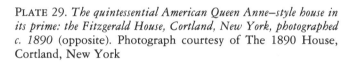

PLATE 30. *The Fitzgerald House, Cortland, New York* (above and right), *as recently repainted in its high-Victorian colors.*

PLATE 29. *The quintessential American Queen Anne–style house in its prime: the Fitzgerald House, Cortland, New York, photographed c. 1890* (opposite). Photograph courtesy of The 1890 House, Cortland, New York

each part striving for supremacy.... Give each [element] its just due, and they will all be quiet; no wrangling; but one beautiful, peaceful, harmonious assemblage, all coming forward with their little gifts, giving them quietly and freely." Two years later, Henry Hudson Holly specifically criticized Downing:

Some years ago it was quite customary to paint houses a sort of dirty yellow, which custom arose from the fact that Mr. Downing, in giving some figurative instructions as to the color employed, said: "Pluck from the ground the roots of the grass, and the color of the earth thereon will be the color of the house." Now, the gist of this was that the color of the house should be in harmony with the landscape; but some of his unimaginative followers failed to see that it was not to be taken literally, and hence arose a fashion which, we are glad to see, has gone by, of painting houses an offensive mud color.[17]

Holly disliked white houses as well; white "is no color at all, always cold and glaring, and making an ugly spot in the landscape: we find nothing to warrant so forcible an intrusion." In cities, Americans should follow the example of the Middle East, "study their picturesque

use of external colors, and let the walls of our cities assume new life and meaning by contrasting tints of various bricks, stones, and brilliant tiles." In the country, lighter tints might be used, but:

I would not have it supposed that positive colors cannot be employed to advantage on the exteriors of country houses. For example, green as the color for the blinds not only has a cool and cheerful effect, but seems to be that chosen by Nature in which to clothe her natural bowers. Still, if neutral tints are used on the body of the house, green is apt to appear in too violent contrast unless a line of some other harmonizing color be interposed. If the general tone of the house is drab or olive, a line of Indian red between this and the blinds would produce a relief. But in coloring our houses it is certainly well to follow the architect's advice, since an improper application of paint might quite nullify the effect of his design, and render that ridiculous which was intended to be dignified; small, that which was to appear large; and obtrusive, that which was to appear modest and retiring.[18]

The movement toward rich tertiary colors that began in the 1870s continued into the 1880s. "The objections

PLATE 31. *The paint scheme of this handsome Queen Anne house photographed c. 1900 retains all the characteristics of high-Victorian color placement: full outlining with dark trim, patterned belt course, roof, and gable shingles, and picking out of frieze panels, turned porch posts, and balusters.* Authors' collection

against employing white for outside purposes," stated the anonymous author of *Every Man His Own Painter!* in 1873, "apply with equal force to other primary colors— they are all too conspicuous and formal in appearance. Yellow is the only one which can be tolerated, and even the shade of that must be carefully selected, or better left alone. Gray also is objectionable, being cold in appearance and especially inappropriate where green is present." According to a writer for F. W. Devoe & Company in the 1880s, this new preference for using rich tertiary colors for exterior decoration developed together with the Queen Anne style:

In its embellished form [the Queen Anne style] admits, without any appearance of incongruity, of the production of the quaintest effects both in the groupings of the parts of a building, the general appearance produced and the working out of the details in the shape of doors, windows, etc. It is, moreover, a form that admits of the most comfortable and attractive

arrangement of the interior, and above all, and what most concerns us, it furnishes an opportunity for the greatest display of taste in coloring and exterior decoration. The many fronts, diversified as to material, with visible framing, shingle or smooth covering, the gables, the porches, etc., all provide a means for the employment of parti-colored effects, the most attractive and artistically valuable features of modern house painting, and one that the old box-pattern house, with its plain flat front, does not so readily admit of.[19]

The color plates in this book clearly show the relationship between the increasing complexity of architecture and the richness of "parti-colored effects"—by which the Victorians meant the use of several colors (see Plates 15, 32, and 33). In *Modern House Painting*, Ehrick Kensett Rossiter and Frank Ayers Wright stated that "the old puritanical hatred of color, which found its natural outcome in white houses with green blinds, has had to give way; at first, to a compromise, in which neutral and

PLATE 32. *This detail of a Queen Anne cottage shows a typical three-color body treatment of the 1880s—Dark Brownstone, Terra Cotta, and Medium Brownstone—unified by two values of Old Gold as the trim that picks out the vertical and horizontal elements. Note the use of black sash throughout.* Sherwin-Williams Company, Color Applied to Architecture (1887). The Athenaeum of Philadelphia Collection

sickly drab tints played a prominent part and, later, to more advanced notions, in which the more positive colors find a chance of expression." The old rule of one body color and a darker trim color no longer applies. "The present style of architecture does not oblige its enforcement, but rather tempts to the use of more colors and a diversified treatment. Where the lines and surfaces are so much broken up as they are now, the old ideas are, indeed, out of place. . . ." The H. W. Johns Company agreed. "New dark body and trimming colors" were added to their line of paint "in consequence of the constantly increasing demand for the new styles of decoration." Johns claimed that it was the first company "to

introduce the rich olive drabs, olive greens, maroons, etc., which are now so effectively and tastefully used in the decoration of ornamental villas, seaside hotels and other structures. . . ."[20]

As the nineteenth century waned, American domestic architecture began to return to simpler lines inspired in part by our colonial past. With this revival, paint colors also changed, as primary and secondary colors began to replace tertiary hues. Body colors moved toward pastels; white again became the most popular trim color and even was used for sash. During the last decade of the century, conflicting points of view concerning how the interior *and* exterior of houses should be decorated vied

PLATE 34. *The Frederick Bunnell House (1888), 507 Whitney Avenue, New Haven, Connecticut, painted appropriately in the style suggested by Plates 32 and 33.*

PLATE 33. *In 1884 the Sherwin-Williams Company published this illustration of "a new and pleasing Queen Anne cottage, where a different color is used in the painting of each story of the house." The ground floor is Dark Brownstone, the second floor Old Gold, and the third floor Amber. "We strongly recommend the use of three body colors for painting this style of architecture; still there are a few {persons} that do not care to keep pace with the improvements in exterior painting, and cling to the old way of using only one color for the entire body of the house." In addition to three body colors, the house was trimmed in Terra Cotta with sash in black or Shutter Green. Sherwin-Williams Company,* House Painting *(1884). The Athenaeum of Philadelphia Collection*

PLATE 35. *The Longfellow House, Cambridge, Massachusetts, as illustrated in its Colonial Revival colors—yellow body, white trim and pilasters, green shutters—by the H. W. Johns Manufacturing Company in* Artistic House Painting *(New York, 1895).* The Athenaeum of Philadelphia Collection

PLATE 36. *Neoclassical trim painted Colonial Revival Ivory against Colonial Revival Blue bodies: from the East Coast (above), and from the West Coast (left).*

for prominence. "Some people want their houses pure white throughout, while others have them painted as dark as possible," observed a housepainter in 1893, "and some peculiar combinations of color are often selected, but we never dare object, or we might lose the job." Critics of the 1890s appeared to favor divergent architectural styles—such as the various revivals and the Arts and Crafts style that ultimately spawned the ubiquitous American bungalow—and paint companies offered paint colors appropriate for the various styles. As early as 1893, the H. W. Johns Company was offering tertiary colors and dark stains for use on late Queen Anne and Shingle-style houses, while simultaneously providing yellows, grays, and blues, "which are so extensively used on Colonial and other styles of houses" that "should be trimmed with our Outside White." For shutters and sash,

the company recommended dark green *or* white. "Body colors of light grays and other neutral tints may also be trimmed with White or Ivory White, using the same color for blinds and sash."[21]

By 1914, firms like the Lowe Brothers Paint Company were recommending that "trimming should be lighter than the house itself . . . , white or very light colors should be used for trim," and "dark colors rarely look well." In this period, nonetheless, the cornice, corner boards, and belt courses (see the glossary, pages 107–109) were still defined against the body color—even when the body was light yellow and the trim an ivory yellowish white. Only later, with the introduction of tract housing, were Americans weaned from multicolor paint schemes and the importance of architectural elements. All these details were lost in a flood of white paint.[22]

PLATE 37. *A typical clapboard and shingle house of the late nineteenth century shown in soft browns and tans with creamy yellow trimmings. Note the Neoclassical "Venetian window" in the attic gable. Both the shutters and the sash are dark green against the painted clapboards of the first floor and the stained shingles above. H. W. Johns Manufacturing Company,* Artistic House Painting *(New York, 1895).* The Athenaeum of Philadelphia Collection

SELECTING COLORS FOR VICTORIAN BUILDINGS

The illustrations in Chapter 2 probably gave you a fairly good idea of where your building falls in the evolving taste for color between 1840 and 1900. And you may already have begun to formulate a color scheme in your mind based partly on your preference for one color or a group of colors and partly on your favorable reaction to one or more of the illustrations in this book, which you might want to flip through before reading this chapter. Still, the problem of selecting the actual colors appears daunting.

Having helped hundreds of homeowners tackle the task of selecting colors, we know how difficult you may imagine the process to be. Homeowners who make the decision to paint in more than one color usually plunge into a great stack of manufacturers' paint sample cards only to thrash around in despair as they try in vain to "select five colors." We've yet to meet an owner—let alone two or more owners attempting to select colors they agree on—who successfully could choose more than one or two colors at the same time. It's like trying to rub your stomach and pat your head while standing on one foot with your eyes closed. In response to this problem, we have gradually evolved a method of walking owners like you through the process in a few relatively painless steps. The steps are the same whether you are painting a pretty cottage in a small Midwestern town or a commercial block in a major city.

Step One. Obtain a full set of colors from one or more of the major national paint manufacturers. Companies such as Sherwin-Williams, Benjamin Moore, Glidden, and Devoe (marketed on the West Coast of the United States as Ameritone Paint) all produce complete bound sets (called "fan decks") of their exterior color lines; however, these sets are not generally given out to individual building owners. Even if your dealer is reluctant to give you a fan deck, he will probably allow you to borrow one long enough to decide which individual cards you want from his free color sample rack. (It is a good idea to avoid the prepackaged lines of "historical" colors that all the manufacturers publish in an effort to ease the pain of color selection; those lines are too limited for your needs.)

Step Two. Table 1 on page 34 lists by name thirty-four common Victorian colors from the period 1840 to 1900. Next to these colors you will find the nearest equivalent color in the four national brands mentioned above. In going through the fan deck of colors you obtained from the dealer, place paper clips on the samples indicated for that brand. In this way, you will have narrowed the available choices to the thirty-four colors that appeared in the paint lines of Victorian manufacturers, as seen in dozens of surviving color cards of the type illustrated in Plate 39 A–F and Plates 24 and 28. If you have more than one fan deck and compare the listed Victorian colors across brands—say, Buff equivalents in Sherwin-Williams and in Benjamin Moore—you will find minor variations. These variations occur because the color lab of every manufacturer uses a different color system and creates its own color formula for use by its retail dealers, who mix the paint by the numbers. Such

PLATE 38. *In an effort to teach theories of "harmonious" combinations, paint companies produced a wide variety of literature featuring color printing and actual chips of paint. This late-nineteenth-century example is from the Sherwin-Williams Company.* The Athenaeum of Philadelphia Collection

---

variations were common in the nineteenth century as well.

Within the limitations of colors available in each modern brand we have made adjustments so that the values remain constant within that brand. Consequently, once you have selected the brand you prefer, do not attempt to match colors across brands. Some manufacturers' color systems provide more of the dark, heavily saturated colors than others do, and in the deep greens and olives, for example, you will probably favor the choice offered by one brand over another. In the lighter colors, differences between brands are minimal. Keep in mind that most full-service paint dealers can blend your colors by visually matching the color samples of a national brand; we have found, however, that the richer colors often defeat the color systems of smaller, regional manufacturers with

limited mixing bases. In addition, if the mixer does not have a sharp eye for color, you may be disappointed with the match.

Step Three. Now comes the only difficult part: selecting from the thirty-four colors those colors that are historically most appropriate for your building. You may want to reread Chapter 2 at this point and look closely at the plates of this book again. Here, for your reference—though not intended to replace the detailed discussion in Chapter 2—is a quick review:

1. Buildings erected prior to the wide distribution of ready-mixed paint (and those in areas of the country where it would have been difficult to obtain ready-mixed paint) should generally be

TABLE 1   VICTORIAN PAINT COLOR NAME EQUIVALENCY

Victorian Term	Sherwin-Williams	Benjamin Moore	Glidden	Devoe
Bronze Green	SW2846	455	80-07	2YO20A
Buff	SW2352	HC-18	78-89	2M58D
Light Drab	SW2066	1523	78-98	not available
Medium Drab	SW2058	1532	79-00	not available
Dark Drab	SW2076	1533	79-02	not available
Fawn	SW2814	HC-16	78-94	2U58B
Shutter Green	SW2809	HC-133	not available	1UM40A
Straw	SW2813	HC-17	78-92	2D58C
Light Gray Stone	SW2136	1486	79-06	2M40E
Medium Gray Stone	SW2134	1488	79-08	2M40D
Dark Gray Stone	SW2138	1489	79-10	2D40C
Light Slate	SW2276	1621	79-55	2M38D
Medium Slate	SW2274	1622	79-57	2D38C
Dark Slate	SW2279	1623	79-59	2U38B
Light Blue Stone	SW2811	699	not available	not available
Dark Blue Stone	SW2810	714	not available	1U25B
Light Blue Green	SW2812	HC-118	not available	1D35C
Dark Blue Green	SW2391	HC-130	not available	1U29B
Light Brownstone	SW2185	1034	78-44	2D44C
Medium Brownstone	SW2183	1035	78-46	2D46C
Dark Brownstone	SW2189	HC-68	78-48	1U47B
Amber	SW2817	189	73-03	2U14B
Indian Red	SW2802	1302	79-66	1VR34A
Old Gold	SW2357	1049	72-79	2YO11A
Light Olive	SW2218	509	74-61	2D24C
Medium Olive	SW2222	510	74-63	not available
Dark Olive	SW2224	511	74-64	1YO25A
Olive Yellow	SW2363	259	73-68	2U21B
Reddish Brown	SW2801	HC-64	79-65	1UM32A
Terra Cotta	SW2803	1218	72-24	2YO31A
Colonial Revival Blue	SW2863	HC-145	77-48	2M37D
Colonial Revival Gray	SW2832	HC-169	79-39	2M39E
Colonial Revival Ivory	SW2833	920	72-73	2H57G
Colonial Revival Yellow	SW2830	293	73-55	2D16C

A

B

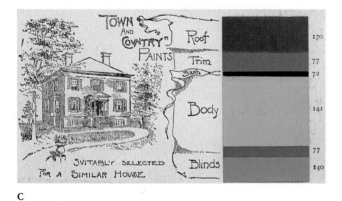

C

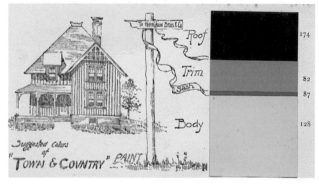

D

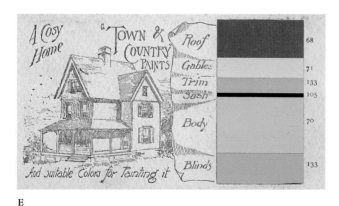

E

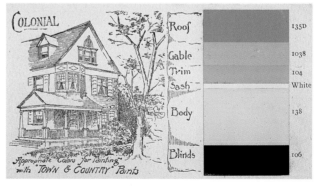

F

PLATE 39. *Selecting appropriate colors for the age and style of the house was as vexing a problem in the nineteenth century as it is today. Harrison Bros. & Co. attempted to assist its customers with this series of cards published in Philadelphia and Chicago, c. 1890. House A is painted Light Olive with Old Gold trim, and both colors were used on the shutters. The gables were "flesh" and the sash black. House B uses Terra Cotta for the body, Amber in the gable, and Indian Red for the trim. The sash is black. A more conservative scheme is applied to house C, employing Straw for a body color, Medium Brownstone for the trim, two shades of Brownstone for the shutters, and black for the sash. For house D the company recommended two shades of Olive with Indian Red sash. House E uses three shades of Slate on the body, trim, and gables, and one on the shutters. House F is painted Buff with the gable in Amber and trim in Light Olive. The shutters are black and the sash white.* The Athenaeum of Philadelphia Collection

painted following the guidelines and the colors recommended by the architects and critics of the picturesque such as Downing, Vaux, and Wheeler. You will be looking at the lighter tints of Fawn, Drab, Straw, Gray Stone, Slate, Brownstone, Buff, Bronze Green, and Shutter Green.

2. Buildings erected after c. 1870 might be painted any of the colors advocated by the critics espousing the picturesque—including the darkest values of Drab, Stone, or Slate—or the rich tertiary colors such as Old Gold, Olive, Olive Yellow, Amber, and Terra Cotta.

3. Late-nineteenth-century buildings in the Colonial Revival style will probably be painted in one of the clear, light colors that became popular again in the 1890s: Colonial Revival Blue, Colonial Revival Gray, Colonial Revival Ivory, and Colonial Revival Yellow.

4. The style, material, and detailing of the structure must also be taken into account. The illustrations in this book and the detailed trimming instruc-

tions in Chapter 4 will give you guidance for selecting colors and determining the *number* of colors. If you have a Queen Anne house, for example, you will probably want to select two or three body colors as well as a trim color. If you are trimming a brick or stucco house you will probably only need one trim color; and so on.

Step Four. Now we begin to select colors. For a frame house you first choose the main body color. This should be a color that you like, and, having narrowed your available choices considerably from the several hundred colors offered by the typical fan deck of a national manufacturer, you should spread out those that remain and make your choice while examining them in *natural daylight*, not under an incandescent or a fluorescent lamp. (Incandescent light enhances the red end of the color spectrum, and most fluorescent lights enhance the blue end of the spectrum; both dramatically alter the way your eye perceives color.)

PLATE 40. *Two views of "an inexpensive country or village house, estimated cost $800," which was "five or ten years ago invariably painted white, with green blinds." In the perspective view (opposite),* the body of the house has been painted Brownstone and the trim Drab. *Note that two additional colors have carefully been introduced for the recessed panels of the shutters and all sash; otherwise the modest trim is not picked out. The front view (right)* illustrates the effect obtained by reversing the colors—the body light and the trim dark. The shutters are painted to match the trim with the sash color used to pick out the first-floor shutter moldings. John Lucas & Co., Portfolio of Modern House Painting Designs *(Philadelphia, 1887).* Dornsife Collection of the Victorian Society in America at the Athenaeum of Philadelphia

Step Five. Having chosen a pleasing body color that is historically appropriate for the age, style, and type of your building, you should then—and only then—turn to Table 2 on page 38, the Color Affinity Chart based upon color schemes recommended by various nineteenth-century books on exterior decoration. You can use this chart to determine which colors the Victorians thought would be the best matches for the body of your building. For example, if you have selected Fawn as the color for the clapboards of your house, Table 2 tells you that the Victorians considered Straw, Buff, Drab, Gray Stone, and Brownstone acceptable trimming colors. If your building requires more than one body or trim color, the table provides several alternatives—for example, you might select Light and Dark Drab. The many alternatives not only make it easier for you to choose your colors but also allow you to express your personal preferences.

Step Six. Having settled on the body color(s) and trim color(s), you will need to determine from Chapter 4 what colors are most appropriate and pleasing for shutters, window sash, porch roof and floor, and any special details such as roof cresting and ironwork, and small

TABLE 2 COLOR AFFINITY CHART
An asterisk following a color name indicates that the match is less successful in some values in some of the modern commercial paint lines.

Bronze Green	A universally applicable color used for roof striping, ironwork, and occasionally for shutters
Shutter Green	A universally applicable shutter color used throughout the nineteenth century
Buff	Straw, Fawn, Medium Stone, Dark Stone, Light Slate, Medium Slate, Dark Slate, Medium Drab, Dark Drab, Old Gold
Light Drab	Medium Drab, Dark Drab, Straw, Fawn, Light Brownstone,* Medium Brownstone, Dark Brownstone, Medium Gray Stone, Dark Gray Stone, Light Slate, Medium Slate, Dark Slate, Old Gold, Light Blue Green,* Dark Blue Green
Medium Drab	Light Drab, Dark Drab, Straw,* Fawn, Buff, Light Brownstone,* Medium Brownstone,* Dark Brownstone, Old Gold
Dark Drab	Light Drab, Medium Drab, Straw, Light Brownstone, Medium Brownstone,* Old Gold, Fawn, Buff
Fawn	Straw, Buff, Light Drab, Medium Drab, Dark Drab, Light Gray Stone,* Medium Gray Stone, Dark Gray Stone, Medium Brownstone,* Dark Brownstone, Dark Blue Green
Straw	Buff, Fawn, Old Gold, Light Drab, Medium Drab,* Dark Drab, Medium Brownstone, Dark Brownstone, Medium Gray Stone, Dark Gray Stone, Light Slate, Medium Slate, Dark Slate, Light Olive, Medium Olive, Dark Olive
Light Gray Stone	Medium Gray Stone, Dark Gray Stone, Light Drab, Medium Drab, Dark Drab, Fawn, Buff, Straw, Old Gold, Light Brownstone, Medium Brownstone, Light Slate, Medium Slate, Dark Slate, Light Blue Stone
Medium Gray Stone	Light Gray Stone, Dark Gray Stone, Light Drab, Medium Drab,* Dark Drab, Fawn, Buff, Straw, Old Gold, Light Brownstone, Medium Brownstone, Dark Brownstone, Light Slate, Medium Slate, Dark Slate, Light Blue Stone, Dark Blue Stone, Dark Blue Green
Dark Gray Stone	Light Gray Stone, Medium Gray Stone, Light Drab, Medium Drab,* Dark Drab,* Light Brownstone, Medium Brownstone, Dark Brownstone, Fawn, Straw, Buff, Old Gold, Light Slate, Dark Slate, Dark Blue Stone, Light Blue Green,* Dark Blue Green
Light Slate	Medium Slate, Dark Slate, Light Drab, Medium Drab, Fawn,* Straw, Buff, Old Gold,* Light Gray Stone, Medium Gray Stone,* Dark Gray Stone
Medium Slate	Light Slate, Dark Slate, Light Drab, Medium Drab, Dark Drab, Fawn, Straw, Buff, Old Gold, Light Gray Stone, Medium Gray Stone, Dark Gray Stone
Dark Slate	Light Slate, Medium Slate, Light Drab, Medium Drab, Dark Drab, Fawn, Straw, Buff, Old Gold, Light Gray Stone, Medium Gray Stone, Dark Gray Stone
Light Blue Stone	Dark Blue Stone, Light Blue Green, Dark Blue Green,* Light Drab, Medium Drab,* Fawn, Buff
Dark Blue Stone	Light Blue Stone, Dark Blue Green,* Light Blue Green,* Medium Drab, Dark Drab, Fawn
Light Blue Green	Dark Blue Green, Light Blue Stone, Dark Blue Stone, Light Drab, Medium Drab, Dark Drab, Buff, Straw, Fawn,* Old Gold*
Dark Blue Green	Light Blue Green, Light Blue Stone,* Dark Blue Stone,* Light Drab, Medium Drab, Dark Drab,* Buff, Straw, Fawn, Old Gold*
Light Brownstone	Medium Brownstone, Dark Brownstone, Light Drab, Medium Drab,* Dark Drab, Light Gray Stone, Medium Gray Stone, Dark Gray Stone, Old Gold
Medium Brownstone	Light Brownstone, Dark Brownstone, Light Drab, Medium Drab,* Dark Drab,* Light Gray Stone, Medium Gray Stone,* Dark Gray Stone, Old Gold,* Fawn*
Dark Brownstone	Light Brownstone, Medium Brownstone, Light Drab, Medium Drab, Light Gray Stone, Medium Gray Stone, Dark Gray Stone, Old Gold, Fawn
Amber (an accent color only)	Terra Cotta, Light Olive, Medium Olive, Dark Olive, Medium Brownstone, Dark Brownstone, Old Gold
Indian Red	A universally applicable color for detail accenting

Old Gold	Light Drab, Medium Drab, Dark Drab, Buff, Straw, Light Brownstone,* Medium Brownstone,* Dark Brownstone, Medium Gray Stone, Dark Gray Stone, Light Olive,* Medium Olive, Dark Olive
Light Olive	Medium Olive, Dark Olive, Reddish Brown, Indian Red (accent), Terra Cotta, Amber,* Olive Yellow, Old Gold, Fawn,* Straw, Buff
Medium Olive	Light Olive, Dark Olive, Reddish Brown, Indian Red (accent), Terra Cotta, Amber, Olive Yellow, Old Gold, Fawn, Straw, Buff
Dark Olive	Light Olive, Medium Olive, Reddish Brown, Indian Red (accent), Terra Cotta, Amber, Olive Yellow, Old Gold, Fawn, Straw, Buff
Olive Yellow	Medium Olive, Dark Olive, Reddish Brown, Fawn, Straw,* Buff, Old Gold
Reddish Brown	Light Olive, Medium Olive, Dark Olive, Straw, Fawn, Old Gold, Terra Cotta, Medium Brownstone, Dark Brownstone
Terra Cotta (an accent color only)	Amber, Light Olive, Medium Olive, Dark Olive, Light Brownstone,* Medium Brownstone, Dark Brownstone
Colonial Revival Blue	Colonial Revival Ivory, Colonial Revival Gray
Colonial Revival Gray	Colonial Revival Ivory, Colonial Revival Blue
Colonial Revival Ivory	Colonial Revival Yellow, Colonial Revival Gray, Colonial Revival Blue
Colonial Revival Yellow	Colonial Revival Ivory, Colonial Revival Gray

details such as porch post chamfers. In Chapter 4 you will find that many of these colors used to pick out particular details are nearly universally applicable, regardless of the colors you selected for the body and trim. Shutter Green and Bronze Green, for example, will work with nearly all color schemes, and the dark greens and Reddish Brown are the most common sash colors when the sash is painted in a color other than the one used for the trim. The general rule of historical painting is that buildings of modest architecture look best with simple paint schemes—few colors and little picking out.

Step Seven. Having selected your colors and made notes from Chapter 4 on detailed placement and accent colors, we recommend that you obtain one can of each major color that you have selected. Since a typical Victorian house can require dozens of gallons of paint, you would be wise to apply a sample of your colors on the building in an area where you can see them all together. A gable is usually the best spot, for body, trim, and sash colors can all be viewed against the sky as a background (Plate 118). Once you have reached this stage, *everyone* will assume you have given permission to pass judgment on your taste—neighbors, in-laws, business associates, the postman, and the newspaper boy will suddenly set themselves up as critics of exterior decoration. The only solace we can offer is a remark made by Calvert Vaux in 1857: "Any person who may wish to have his residence judiciously painted will do well to depend on himself to make the selection of colors: and if he will but study the matter simply and fairly, trusting to his real natural instinctive taste, and will regulate his decision by his private feeling for what is agreeable or otherwise, instead of by what he finds next door to him, he will at once cut loose from conventional absurdity, and probably arrive at a result that will be artistic and pleasing."[1]

COLOR PLACEMENT ON VICTORIAN BUILDINGS

Now that you have selected colors for your house, you need to consider how to apply those colors to enhance the design, in the manner intended by the original designer, builder, and owners. This chapter, which discusses in some detail color placement and finishing techniques, including sanding, graining, and roof striping, will help you achieve that goal. In our discussions of color placement and finishing techniques, we sometimes use architectural terminology with which you may not be familiar; for that reason we have supplied a glossary on pages 107–109.

ROOFS

Like most old-house owners, you probably pay little attention to the roof over your head until it leaks—or until you decide to paint your old house in a multicolor paint scheme. Then you begin to realize that the typical Victorian house roof may be as extensive in area and appearance as the siding. Too often houses are reroofed without thought as to how the roof color will relate to the siding and trim colors; then the owners discover that their ideal color scheme no longer will work. Consequently, you must take the roof into account when planning to paint.

As a general rule, the original roofs of Victorian houses were slate, wooden shingle, metal, or ceramic tile. The color range was somewhat limited: Slate appears purple, gray black, blue black, red, or green; wooden shingles

(unless they are painted or stained) mellow to brown or gray; and most seamed metal roofs—the fire-resistant alternative to shingles but not as heavy as slate—require painting. Terra cotta tiles, which became popular in the late nineteenth and early twentieth century, are usually yellow to brownish red if unglazed. (Occasionally, early-twentieth-century Mediterranean Revival and other post-Victorian structures are roofed in glazed tiles that may be bright red, green, or blue.) Whether you select one of these historical roofing materials or one of the durable and economical modern substitutes, you need to simulate the colors of the historical materials to achieve an appropriate overall paint scheme. Let's examine some of the alternatives.[1]

Slate has long been valued in America as a superior roofing material—although, prior to the opening of American quarries, most slate was imported from Wales. Slate is fireproof, durable, relatively maintenance free, and visually handsome. It is also expensive to install, frustrating to repair, and its weight may strain a structure not specifically designed for such a heavy load. Nonetheless, by the mid-nineteenth century the opening of American quarries and the digging of canals and laying of railroads made slate available to supply the burgeoning demand for decorative roofs on American villas and cottages.[2]

A surviving slate roof should be repaired or replaced with slates of the original texture and color. The color of the slate may influence the paint colors you choose for the building, but most slate visually "reads" as neutral

PLATE 41. *Ornamental sawed wooden shingles contribute greatly to the picturesque roof line of this 1881 Queen Anne seaside cottage with a Boutique paint scheme.*

PLATE 42. *Special effects normally associated with historical slate roofs can be reproduced with modern asphalt shingles, as shown here on the Gothic Revival McCreary House (1869–70) in Cape May, New Jersey, now operated as the Abbey Inn.*

PLATE 43. *The exterior decoration of seaside Victorian cottages was often festive. Shown here is the Samuel D. Robinson cottage at Oak Bluffs, site of a Methodist campground on Martha's Vineyard, Massachusetts (c. 1890). Notice in particular the two-color roof shingles and the exuberant trim on the porches and balconies. Both cottages have wonderful roof crestings.* Photograph courtesy of the Society for the Preservation of New England Antiquities

PLATE 44. *An acroterion is the decorative feature at the apex of a roof pediment that is commonly found in Neoclassical architecture and occasionally on vernacular Victorian cottages. This one in the form of a stylized acanthus leaf has been picked out in the body color rather than painted to blend with the trim color used on the cornice. For a nineteenth-century photograph documenting this practice see Plate 43.*

PLATE 45. *The darker colors of the 1880s generally make a house appear smaller, especially when the vertical and horizontal trimmings are carefully picked out, as on this villa in "a sort of an Americanized Gothic style." The house is Dark Olive trimmed in Old Gold and Terra Cotta on the bargeboards, scalloped friezes, and porch brackets, with just a touch of Indian Red picking out. "The frilled drapery," wrote Elisha C. Hussey in* Home Building . . . from New York to San Francisco *(New York, 1876), "passes entirely around the gables and eaves, effectually breaking up the harshness so common to straight cornice lines. . . ." Notice how important the two-color slate roof is to the entire composition. Also study closely the reversal of body and trim colors on the window bay, which adds "very much to the exterior richness of effect." Seeley Bros. Paint Company (New York, 1886).* Collection of Mr. and Mrs. Lewis Seeley, The Athenaeum of Philadelphia

DIMENSION SHINGLES.

ORNAMENTAL ENDS.

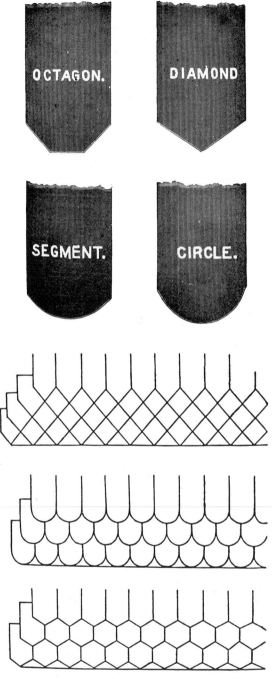

PLATE 46. *"Ornamental" sawed shingles available in 1892 from the Foster-Munger Company of Chicago (top). Sawed wooden shingles began to replace traditional hand-split shingles early in the nineteenth century, and A. J. Downing argued, "some character is given to the roof . . . by employing shingles of a uniform size, and rounding the lower ends before laying them on the roof." He illustrated several patterns in* The Architecture of Country Houses *(New York, 1850) (below). The Athenaeum of Philadelphia Collection*

and need not dominate your choice of the color scheme for the building—just as Bronze Green or reddish brown colors were recommended for standing seam metal roofs regardless of the colors suggested for the siding or trim. If the roof is totally replaced with new slate, the color choices are blue gray, blue black, and black (from Pennsylvania quarries); red (New York); green, light gray, and purple (Vermont); and blue gray to dark gray (Virginia). During the nineteenth century, several colors of slate were occasionally used on the same roof to create decorative patterns similar to that shown in Plate 45. If you attempt to re-create such a pattern, you could pick up the second slate color as a trim color for the house.[3]

Wooden shingles, sometimes having ornamental ends that created interesting patterns (see Plates 46, 47, and 48), appear on many American Victorian houses, either as the principal roofing material, as overall siding, or as one of several decorative alternatives on the multitextured Queen Anne Revival structures of the last quarter of the nineteenth century. Most Victorian painting guides recommended staining or painting roof shingles dark red, dark reddish brown, or dark olive green. In their 1884 promotional book *House Painting*, the Sherwin-Williams Company argued, "Shingles not only last enough longer to repay the painting, but painting the roof of a house gives a fine opportunity to get a good color effect and completes the picture." Ehrick Kensett Rossiter and Frank Ayers Wright stated in *Modern House Painting* that a shingled roof "can be painted red or stained a reddish brown," and according to Sherwin-Williams "a roof should not be painted a light color, but some dark color that will strongly contrast with the paint on the main part of the building." Even as late as 1920 the National Lead Company told readers of *The House We Live In*, "The roofs of bungalows are nearly always in strong, dark colors—venetian red and olive green for instance."[4]

Metal roofs often present the biggest problem because the original roofs have rarely survived, and it is difficult to find qualified craftsmen able to reproduce the historical surface. The most universally popular American metal roof of the nineteenth century was tinplate, a generic term for rolled *iron* plates coated with tin, lead, an alloy of lead and tin, or zinc—all designed to protect the iron from rusting. Light in weight, durable, and inexpensive compared to slate, imported English tinplate was applied to thousands of American buildings. (American tinplate did not supersede the English product until the protectionist McKinley Tariff of 1890 was passed.) The coated iron plates (14 inches × 20 inches to 20 inches × 28 inches) were joined into rolls with flat seams, hoisted onto the roof, and joined by "standing" seams, thereby creating parallel lines running from ridge to eaves that were occasionally treated decoratively (see pages 46–50).[5]

PLATE 47. *The dramatic effect of a red painted roof of ornamental sawed wooden shingles is clearly evident on the recently restored mansard roof of the Second Empire–style Queen Victoria Inn in Cape May, New Jersey.*

PLATE 48. *Ornamental shingles being applied to the mansard roof of a cottage in Cape May, New Jersey. Andrew Jackson Downing remarked that "a very pleasing effect is produced, at little extra cost, by introducing three or four courses of these ornamental shingles between several courses of plain shingles. . . . A very little additional labour in this way bestows an air of taste on a common roof."* The Architecture of Country Houses *(New York, 1850).*

Just as many Victorian houses have suffered the visual indignity and potential long-term damage of being re-sided with asphalt, asbestos, aluminum, or even plastic, so too original metal roofs that began to leak have often been recoated with materials that are tar-paper black or barn-roof silver. These ugly smears or bright flashes draw the eye away from what otherwise might be a successful paint scheme. Such roofs should be painted over or should be replaced by new materials of a color compatible with the rest of the house.

All nineteenth-century architects agreed that a new tinplate roof had to be painted on both sides (to prevent rusting through from underneath) and that the exposed surface was to be repainted regularly—usually every four years—with iron oxide and linseed oil, a mixture dark red or dark brownish red in color. In *How Shall We Paint Our Houses?* John Masury remarked, "Where the roof is a conspicuous object in the architecture of the building, a dark color be indispensable, the use of pure Venetian Red, darkened with Lamp Black, is rec-ommended as the most durable and economical." If you reroof your building in modern plated steel, you need to select a roof color; newly applied steel is brightly metallic and must be painted to simulate a historical roof.[6]

Nineteenth-century painting guides illustrate a vari-ety of colors for metal roofs, but most called for painting in dark red, dark reddish brown (the iron oxide colors mentioned above), or a dark olive green. (The moderate red called "roofer's" red derives from this tradition, but it may be too bright for use with most historical paint schemes. It should be cut by the addition of some black prior to application.) Copper roofs, of course, do not require painting and develop a handsome patina natu-rally.[7]

Finally, if slate, wooden shingles, standing seam metal, or tiles are simply too expensive, you may decide that modern composition roofing of asphalt or fiberglass is your only practical alternative. While these materials rarely simulate the *texture* of the original roof, you can at least select a color close to one of those mentioned above.

Tent Roofs and Awnings

The painting of veranda roofs is one aspect of roof treat-ment that needs more detailed discussion. To under-stand the problem, look closely at the simple frame house from Mauricetown, New Jersey, shown in Plate 50. The owners have selected attractive, historically ap-propriate colors and placed them with skill. But notice how the façade is spoiled by the black smear of the asphalt roof. During the mid-nineteenth century, such

porches—or verandas, as they were called during that period—were usually roofed with metal that curved like the canvas awning of a military campaign tent. To heighten this illusion of canvas, the roof typically was painted in stripes of alternating colors, "to relieve the monotonous effect of the uniform surface." This decorative technique is sometimes difficult for modern owners to accept, yet historical documents strongly suggest the widespread application of the treatment.[8]

Fortunately we have both written and pictorial doc-umentation for the colors of striped roofs. In 1849 the Philadelphia architect John Notman designed an Ital-ianate villa for Isaac Pearson, and a full set of detailed specifications—although not the house—have survived. "The whole of the wood work as usually painted will have 3 coats of white lead and oil of best quality," Not-man wrote. "The last coat on the shutters to be green . . . the sash and frames will be painted stone col-our outside, the porch and bow window to be sanded, *the roof of the balcony to be painted in stripes bronze and pale yellow, the iron work of bronze.*" Notman's roof treatment is similar to the green and yellow combination dating from 1861 shown in Plate 52 from John Riddell's

| 87 | 121 | 144 | 150 | 617 | Grey | 73 | 169 |

See Description.

PLATE 49. *Cresting such as that found on the conical roof of the Queen Anne–style Haas-Lilienthal House (Peter R. Schmidt, architect, 1886) in San Francisco (opposite) might be painted Bronze Green or to match the main trim color of the house. Decorative roof cresting of terra cotta tiles appears in this illustration (above) from* House Painting and Decorating *(December 1885). The complex paint scheme includes three body colors—Dark Brownstone, Fawn, and Amber—trimmed in Medium and Light Brownstone, with sash painted Indian Red.* The Athenaeum of Philadelphia Collection

PLATE 50. *A vernacular cottage with a tent roof. The black roof surface cries out to be striped—and, in fact, was striped after this photograph was taken.*

PLATE 51. *The striped veranda roof at The Athenaeum of Philadelphia, designed by John Notman, 1847.*

FRONT ELEVATION.

PLATE 52. *This "neat and convenient homestead" in the Italianate Revival style cost $5,150 to erect on the eve of the Civil War. It illustrates several important details: green blinds (shutters) on the second floor, oak-grained front door, striped porch roof, light-colored sash, and sidelight frames (on either side of the front door), which may have been intended for graining. Notice how the green of the blinds is used on the scalloped trim to cover the porch flashing (joining porch and roof to side wall) and also the color contrast of the stucco quoins on the corners. The banding of the lantern (enclosed belvedere) trim is an interesting detail that enlivens the entire composition. John Riddell,* Architectural Details for Model Country Residences *(Philadelphia, 1861).* The Athenaeum of Philadelphia Collection

PLATE 53. *The permanent hood of the tower balcony was painted in stripes to match the canvas awnings at Nuits, the residence of F. Cottenet near Dobbs Ferry, New York.* Villas on the Hudson *(New York, 1860).* Dornsife Collection of the Victorian Society in America at The Athenaeum of Philadelphia

PLATE 54. *Several ways of mounting canvas awnings are suggested in this illustration of a late-nineteenth-century house* (opposite). *This house, with its late Victorian tower and comfortable Colonial Revival veranda, appears to be painted Buff or Straw and trimmed with Bronze Green, which is also used on the sash and shutters.* H. W. Johns Manufacturing Company, Artistic House Painting *(New York, 1895).* The Athenaeum of Philadelphia Collection

Architectural Designs for Model Country Residences. Riddell remarked, "all the tin of the roofs is to receive three good coats of good paint, one on the underside before put on, and two on the upper side; *the roof of the veranda is to be striped*; all the lower story doors, and front sash, are to be grained in oak, pivot blinds and wire screens to be green. . . ." Since cast-iron veranda supports are almost always specified to be Bronze Green, the same color commonly appears as one of the striping colors. The second striping color is then taken from the main body or trim color of clapboard houses or the color of the brick or stucco of masonry houses. So popular was Bronze Green that Alexander Jackson Davis recommended the color—perhaps to imitate aged copper—for the entire tinplate roofs of houses illustrated in his *Rural Residences.*[9]

The width of the stripes varies from approximately a foot for large veranda roofs down to four to six inches for small balcony roofs. Standing seams are typically about one foot apart; therefore, you will find the painting a simple matter of following the seam lines, working outward from the center pair of stripes. If there are no seams to follow, or they are too far apart, you will have to snap chalk lines. Narrow striping is well illustrated in the c. 1860 photograph of a New York house from *Villas on the Hudson* (Plate 53) where the tent roof of the balcony and the canvas awnings are clearly *en suite*; the painted stripes, probably olive green and a light stone color to match the trim, appear to be the same width and colors as those of the fabric.[10]

Awnings were a common feature of both residential and commercial Victorian buildings. Today we are seeing a revival of awnings, not only for historical and aesthetic reasons but because they save energy, provide protection from the weather, and reduce the damaging effects of the sun's rays on carpets and curtains. Even an air-conditioned building can stay 10 to 15 degrees cooler through the use of awnings, resulting in a substantial saving on air-conditioning costs. Needless to say, *aluminum* awnings are inappropriate on any building erected prior to World War II. Traditional canvas is still the best material to use, offering the widest range of colors; most modern fabrics often have a shiny finish that detracts from the appearance of a building.[11]

THE CHIMNEY

Masonry chimneys are usually painted the same color as the main body of the structure. A house of soft brick painted yellow, for example, would most likely have a yellow chimney. If your chimney is rebuilt during restoration, you may neglect to paint it, perhaps because you are reluctant to paint over your brand-new and expensive brick chimney. Nonetheless, an unpainted red-brick chimney projecting through the roof of a yellow-painted brick house is incongruous.

HALF-TIMBER GABLES

Half-timbering is encountered in the Tudor, Gothic, and English Cottage revival styles erected between the 1890s and the 1920s. The original medieval buildings that inspired these styles had exposed timbers that were structural supports of the frame and roof; the spaces between the timbers were filled with lime plaster or rough-cast sand stucco, stone, or brick. When painting half-timbering you should take into consideration its historical origins, and paint the frames to look like weathered oak: black, dark brown, or, perhaps, dark green or olive.

If the masonry between the exposed timbers is natural brick, the area may be left alone. However, if the brick has been painted, you should remove the paint or simply paint over in dark red or dark brown to match the original brick color. When the material between the framing timbers is stucco it should be painted white—to suggest the lime-rich plastering that is naturally white—or cream or yellow—to represent one of the river sand stuccoes. On rare occasions in the nineteenth century when the sand used was of a reddish cast, the stucco assumed a faint rose-beige tint.

SHINGLED GABLES

As the nineteenth century advanced, wooden shingles became increasingly popular as siding, and it is not uncommon to find them used well into the twentieth cen-

PLATE 56. *Post-Centennial fascination with early English architectural motifs spawned the ubiquitous Queen Anne style and other variations drawn from Tudor, Elizabethan, and Jacobean periods. (In the twentieth century such motifs as half-timbering would reappear in hundreds of "Stockbroker Tudor" developments.) This complexly painted example uses Straw and Terra Cotta for body colors, Dark Brownstone for trim and Amber for the sash.* House Painting and Decorating (August 1886). The Athenaeum of Philadelphia Collection

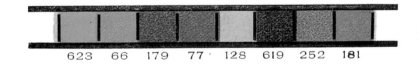

623   66   179   77   128   619   252   181

PLATE 55. *Notice how the body and trim colors—Straw, Medium Brownstone, and Fawn—have been used on the chimney shaft of this Second Empire–style, mansard-roofed house. Also, in contrast to the villa shown in Plate 2, which is picked out in bright red, the color introduced here is a much deeper shade. We are told that "the piazzas incline to plainness, the main cornice is moderately ornamented, and the deck is set with small brackets, and carries over it an iron cresting and finials, which greatly embellishes it, and breaks up all harshness of the skylines." Body and trim colors are reversed in the conventional manner, but the touch of dark red shows on the dormer console brackets, cornice bracket faces, the scalloped frieze in the cornice, the patera below each bracket, and the sash. Seeley Bros. Paint Company (New York, 1886).* Collection of Mr. and Mrs. Lewis Seeley, The Athenaeum of Philadelphia

Design Nº 31
SMALL COUNTRY HOUSE
PAINTED WITH
Harrisons'
"TOWN AND COUNTRY"
Ready Mixed Paints.
HAZLEHURST & HUCKEL · Architects·
Philadelphia ·

PLATE 57. *A clapboard and shingle "Small Country House" with half-timbered gable and Colonial Revival detailing by the Philadelphia architects Edward P. Hazelhurst and Samuel Huckel, Jr., is shown here in eleven colors: foundation, base of the first story, body of the first story, body of the second story (two colors), gables (two colors), trim, sash, roof, and chimney. "Town and Country Ready Mixed Paints," Harrison Bros. & Co., Philadelphia (c. 1884).* Collection of Mr. and Mrs. Edward D. Dart, The Athenaeum of Philadelphia

tury. O. C. Harn, writing in *Correct Color Schemes* for the National Lead Company of Pittsburgh, stated: "Houses with shingled upper stories as a rule should be painted on the lower story a lighter shade than the shingles. The shingles may be indian red, dark brown, dark green or some olive shade. The body should harmonize, as light or dark olive with indian red, cream with browns, the grays with dark green or dull red."[12]

The triangular space created by the gable of a double-sloping roof—called the *tympanum*, in architectural terminology—was often covered in shingles, even when they were not used elsewhere on the structure (see Plate 58). While an *unshingled* tympanum is usually painted the main body color, the presence of interestingly shaped shingles generally signals that the original designer in-

tended a change in both texture and color. On large Queen Anne Revival structures, the gable tympanum is usually painted a third body color (see Plate 33), but even in more modest, vernacular houses, this space allowed for the introduction of a second body color. In the 1880s, the Sherwin-Williams Company described the amber color in its line as "not generally used as a body color for the plain class of buildings where the entire body is of one color, but is very useful in the modern Queen Anne and Swiss structures for second story, gables or roofs, when other colors are in good contrast." Common tympanum colors were yellow, terra cotta, and orange. You should take care not to paint the tympanum so dark as to make the house look top-heavy; instead, use a light and fairly positive color. And one

PLATE 58. *After c. 1880 the Queen Anne style was gradually replaced by the Shingle style—with which it shared some common motifs—a transition apparent at Clearview Farm House, home of paint manufacturer George D. Wetherill in Bellevue, Delaware. Note that the stone foundation color has been used as the principal shingle color, which looks to be Slate or Gray Stone, but Buff has been used as a second body color on the tympanum. The trim is Fawn. Atlas Ready-Mixed Paint Company (Philadelphia, c. 1890).* The Athenaeum of Philadelphia Collection

last warning: Even when different patterns of shaped shingles appear in the tympanum, there is little nineteenth-century evidence for the use of more than one color. Picking out each section of the pattern in a different color is done only as part of a Boutique paint scheme.[13]

BARGEBOARDS

Bargeboards (also called gableboards, vergeboards, or face rafters) are trim elements that hang from the projecting ends of gable roofs (see Plate 59). When painting bargeboards, you should follow historical painting practice: the simpler the board, the simpler the painting.

Thus, you should paint unornamented bargeboards in the main trim color to match the cornice, corner boards, etc., to continue the outline of the house.

Occasionally the faces of these boards are decorated with panels, moldings, or even low relief carving. (Low relief carving is usually found on the bargeboards of houses erected c. 1900 that are heavily influenced by early English and Alpine European sources.) Such carving should never be picked out so that it stands in sharp relief against its background. Rather, it should be painted in the same dark colors suggestive of aged oak that are recommended above for Tudor Revival, half-timbered structures. When the bargeboards are enlivened by panels, applied ornaments, or moldings, you can on a clapboard house reintroduce the principal body color. On masonry

PLATE 59. *Simple bargeboards with applied moldings that have been successfully picked out with the body color against the trim color.*

PLATE 60. *In the 1880s, the Heath & Milligan Manufacturing Company of Chicago issued sample books of "fashionable tints" to show "the appearance of a house when painted with any of our shades." This house is a relatively simple vernacular box that has been enriched by incised decoration on the window frames, belt course, and bargeboards. The colors shown here—a Light Stone gray, Drab trimmings, and an Indian Red roof—illustrate how persistent the colors advocated by Downing in the 1840s proved to be, especially on simple buildings.* The Athenaeum of Philadelphia Collection

houses, you can use a lighter or darker value of the trim color to heighten the contrast. Keep in mind, however, that when the trim of a masonry structure is painted a stone color and sanded to simulate carved stone, it would be inappropriate to introduce a second color.

GUTTERS AND DOWNSPOUTS

Eave gutters and downspouts that carry rainwater and snow melt off roofs were less common in the nineteenth century than they are today. Yet inadequate guttering is second only to failed roofs as the cause of cornice rot and paint failure. You *must* repair or replace gutters and downspouts before preparing the surface for repainting. *Paint applied to damp wood or to surfaces constantly subjected to dripping roof water will fail immediately.*

Like storm windows, modern metal gutters and downspouts are often available from local distributors in white only, and their application to a house with trim and body colors other than white can ruin the appearance of the most carefully planned and applied color scheme. Therefore, gutters and downspouts should be painted to make

them as inconspicuous as possible. On a frame house with olive trim and a light green body, for example, the gutters would probably be painted olive to disappear against the olive cornice, but the downspouts would be painted light green if they crossed the siding. However, if the downspouts followed the corner boards on their way to the ground they would continue in the olive color of the corner boards.

On masonry buildings the downspouts are often found painted Bronze Green to simulate weathered copper, regardless of the brick, stone, or stucco color. True copper downspouts on both masonry and clapboard structures should be allowed to oxidize naturally, regardless of the color of the building.

SANDED PAINT

Another special finish used by the Victorians is sanded paint. This is an optional treatment—and one you may well decide you'd rather not attempt—but since the technique is mentioned throughout this chapter, it needs to be explained now.

Once you realize that much nineteenth-century ex-

PLATE 61. *Sanded paint is normally found on the wood trim of masonry buildings. At Fountain Elms, a mid-nineteenth-century Italianate Revival house by the architect William Woollett in Utica, New York, both the stucco walls and the wood trim were originally sanded. This finish was restored in 1984.* Photograph by Gale R. Farley, courtesy of the Munson-Williams-Proctor Institute

terior decoration of wooden and cast-iron buildings was intended to simulate stone, the choice of colors—especially for masonry buildings—becomes much easier to understand and to copy today. The abundant availability of forest products made wooden framing the least expensive material for residential construction in most parts of North America; but this did not prevent our forefathers from attempting to make their buildings *appear* to be constructed of substantial, expensive, and presumably more desirable masonry. As the historical

finishes of American eighteenth- and nineteenth-century buildings are reexamined by specialists using modern scientific techniques, we have gradually realized that sand was commonly mixed with or blown onto painted surfaces to preserve the finish and to simulate stone.

Even those house-proud Americans George Washington and Thomas Jefferson were not above a little visual conceit, especially when it also proved practical. Listen to George Washington writing to the architect William Thornton from Mount Vernon in 1799: "Sanding, is designed to answer two purposes, durability, and presentation of Stone; for the latter purpose, and in my opinion a desirable one; it is the last operation, by dashing, as long as any will stick, the Sand upon a coat of thick paint. This is the mode I pursued with the painting at this place. . . ." Jefferson also sanded his early-nineteenth-century porticoes at Monticello, just as George Washington had earlier sanded the wooden siding and veranda at Mount Vernon. Nor is this a Southern aberration; to the north, in Newport, Rhode Island, the amateur architect Peter Harrison designed the Redwood Library (1748) after a Roman Doric temple—complete with portico and wings—which was built entirely of rusticated wood (that is, wood cut to look like blocks of stone) and in the late eighteenth century sanded to imitate stone.[14]

In the nineteenth century, painters often simulated stone by sanding the paint applied to cornices, window surrounds, door frames, and porch details. In 1837, Alexander Jackson Davis specified that the "bay-windows, and oriel, of wood," on one of his designs be "painted and dusted with pulverized marble," and the English architect Gervase Wheeler—whose spotty career in America spanned the decade immediately prior to the Civil War—wrote that dashing sand onto freshly applied paint or mixing sand into the paint prior to application, "besides assisting in its preservation, takes away from the oily glare and glisten of ordinary pigments, and by lessening the refracting power, gives to the surface of the building a softer and more pleasant tone of coloring."[15]

Andrew Jackson Downing generally disliked making

PLATE 62. *When the deteriorating and unsafe brownstone porches of the Italianate Revival Morse-Libby House were recently replicated in wood, the new surfaces were painted and sanded to match the stone—a time-honored technique given a new use in restoration. This splendid c. 1860 house in Portland, Maine, by architect Henry Austin, is now a museum open to the public.* Photographs courtesy of the Victoria Society of Maine

wood look like stone, favoring truthfulness of materials. However, in *The Architecture of Country Houses* he allowed for its use in some circumstances: "Perhaps an exception may be allowed in the case of wooden verandas, and such light additions to buildings of solid materials as we often see added in this country, in districts where the stone is so hard as to be very costly when wrought into small parts, so that wood is often used, but is so painted and sanded as to harmonize with the stone. In this case, we say, the apparent untruthfulness is permissible. . . ."[16]

Victorian paint manufacturers confirmed the widespread use of sanded finishes by including sanded samples on their color cards. For example, look at the card of "Homestead Colors" produced by F. W. Devoe & Company in the late 1860s (Plate 24). Colors 24, 33,

and 15 are shown "sanded" to simulate Nova Scotia Stone, Brown or Free Stone, and Ohio Sand Stone. As Washington and Downing suggested above, sanding is normally used to simulate sedimentary "freestone"— such as limestone or sandstone—that can be wrought by mallet and chisel or sawed and turned, as opposed to the denser metamorphic rocks, such as granite, which must be dressed with pointed tools and therefore are more difficult and expensive to work for small-scale residential trimmings.[17]

While any painted surface can be sanded to simulate freestone, Downing's admonition to sand only "wooden verandas, and such light additions to buildings of solid materials," should be honored. Based on the microanalysis of structures such as Fountain Elms—a stuccoed Italianate villa erected in 1850–1852 in Utica, New

PLATE 63. *A recently renovated cast-iron façade in Philadelphia. Such commercial architecture was commonly painted to simulate brownstone, limestone, or marble and then sanded to heighten the illusion. The colors shown here (not sanded) are historical, although applied in a manner more appropriate to a residential structure—a demure commercial "painted lady."* Photograph courtesy of the Devoe Group

PLATE 64. *High-Victorian color schemes for two commercial buildings—one brick and one frame—of a type surviving by the thousands in all parts of America. On the brick storefront, the Sherwin-Williams Company suggested the use of a Dark Olive on posts and panels, and on the remainder a lighter grayish olive; the body of the second and third stories were Reddish Brown; the window caps and cornice in grayish olive; the sash black, the moldings dark reddish brown; the sign in gold and black. On the wooden building next door, the first floor is Dark Olive Green, the body of the second story Medium Olive Green, the trim Light Olive Green, and the sash Reddish Brown. Sherwin-Williams Company,* House Painting: The Best Materials and Methods, Harmony of Colors and Correct Combinations *(Cleveland, 1884).* The Athenaeum of Philadelphia Collection

PLATE 65. *Brick façades in Lexington, Kentucky, recently repainted in historical colors as part of a block-square revitalization sponsored by private investors.* Photograph courtesy of the Webb Companies

York—and the Ebenezer Maxwell Mansion—a stone house erected in 1859 in Germantown, Pennsylvania—sanding is usually found on the wooden elements trimming masonry structures or on the siding of frame buildings where the wood has been shaped to simulate stone. At Woodside, a stuccoed late Neoclassical house near Richmond, Virginia, the 1858 specifications directed the "Cornices, Porches, front & rear Lintels, frames &c to be painted and sanded in imitation of light brown sand stone (Cornice to be kept a few shades darker)."[18]

In the second half of the nineteenth century, when cast-iron building elements in cut, turned, or carved stone shapes became widely used for both residential and commercial construction, painters began to sand these as well—particularly the prefabricated, cast-iron fronts of commercial buildings. Having stated this rule,

it is appropriate to quote Gervase Wheeler again before moving on to discuss the actual process of sand painting: "I do not recommend this process in all cases . . . ," he wrote in 1851. "Sometimes one sees iron sanded in imitation of stone;—many area railings in New York are so finished,—he would be a cunning mason who could cut such splinters of Connecticut brown-stone!"[19]

When restoring the historical exterior decoration of museum structures such as Mount Vernon, Monticello, and Fountain Elms, scientific authenticity is required; microanalysis is used to determine the basic paint color and then grading of the sand by geologic type, ratio of granule size, and color. This kind of rigorous effort to determine and simulate the historical finish is essential because the color and granule size will affect the look of the final application. Washington tells us he used "freestone" that had been crushed and sifted to get a uniform sand. Jefferson, however, appears to have used sand from the nearby Rivanna River with granules of widely varying sizes to simulate light brown sandstone. Gervase Wheeler warned in 1855 that the color "will be changed by the addition of sand. . . . The finest and whitest sand that the neighborhood affords should be used, and as its hue differs so will the tint of the paint be changed."[20]

Of course, Historical-level authenticity appropriate for most privately owned Victorian buildings does not demand the expensive analyses required for landmark museum buildings. If your house is of masonry—or constructed of wood or cast iron designed to simulate masonry—choose a base color as close as possible to the natural color of the simulated stone, as suggested by the Devoe color card reproduced in Plate 24. If your building has actual stone trimmings—door and window lintels, water table and belt course, foundation, or quoins—it is appropriate and highly desirable to custom-blend your paint to match a cleaned sample of these so the overall trim of the building will be unified. According to Gervase Wheeler, a brick house with windows and chimneys trimmed in stone could be "painted and sanded a deep, warm cream color, with those parts of the building which are constructed of wood, painted the same tone of color, but of deeper tint." Lacking such examples for guidance, you might select a color from the stone trim of a nearby structure of the same age. Wheeler believed that the ideal harmony for a building with masonry walls—be they stone, brick, or stucco—would be "obtained by the wood-work being sanded to protect from the weather, and painted to suit the tone of coloring of the stone."[21]

As Wheeler also warned, the color and texture of the sand itself is critical, and this may prove difficult for the modern owner. Gray or light brownstones are fairly easy to simulate today with washed and sifted sand available from building supply dealers; keep in mind that the finer the sand granules, the more like cut stone your job will appear. If you wish to simulate the deeply colored sandstones or brownstones, however, it will be necessary to use garnet sands available from dealers specializing in commercial abrasives.

Fortunately, it is not necessary to stand in the yard throwing handfuls of sand at your freshly painted house—as Washington directed his architect to do—and convincing a professional painter to do so might prove difficult. In most cases the sand can be rapidly and evenly applied with an inexpensive glitter gun attached to an air compressor. Before actually starting on the trim of your building, you should practice on some scrap wood of similar sizes and shapes. This will allow you or your painter to adjust the color and texture of the application while learning, first, the optimum distance from the surface to hold the glitter gun and, second, the proper wetness of the surface to obtain the best coverage. Normally you will have to allow the paint to dry for about ten minutes before you attempt to apply the sand. Fluctuations of temperature and humidity will affect how quickly the work can proceed, and you may find that sanding can be done only while the area being worked is in the shade.[22]

After the surface to be sanded has been prepared and primed, the first coat of *oil-base paint* is brushed on (latex paint will not work for sanding). While the surface is still wet the sand is applied and then allowed to dry thoroughly before repeating the process a second time. Two coats—both sanded—will give you a more stone-like effect, although you may be content with a single application over a prime coat.

One final cautionary note: A sand finish is every bit as durable as Washington, Downing, and Wheeler said; if properly applied it will last far longer than comparable flat painting. Because of this quality, however, it is virtually impossible to remove.

PLATE 66. *A sanded column base at Thomas Jefferson's Monticello near Charlottesville, Virginia, as recently restored. Compare this illustration with Plate 62, bottom, for the dramatic range of colors and textures that can be simulated by sanding.* Photograph by H. Andrew Johnson, courtesy of the Thomas Jefferson Memorial Foundation, Inc.

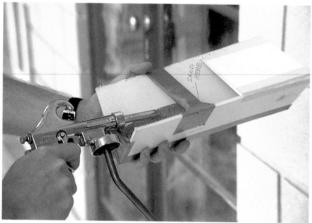

PLATE 67. *Sanding the rusticated portico at Monticello, and a close-up of the trough developed on the site to hold the sand when granular sizes were too large for the glitter gun.* Photographs courtesy of the Thomas Jefferson Memorial Foundation, Inc.

CORNICES

The *cornice* of a building is its exterior trim at the point where walls and roof meet. In classical architecture the cornice is one element of the *entablature* (consisting of the architrave, frieze, and cornice). In lay terms, the entablature is the horizontal element between the tops of columns on a classical building and its roof. The cornice of most Victorian buildings (see the glossary, pages 107–109) is composed of 1) a simple bed molding that separates the cornice from the side wall; 2) the soffit, which is the exposed *underside* of the cornice; 3) the fascia, a flat horizontal band; and 4) the decorative crown molding, directly under the roof. How these elements of the cornice are painted depends on their complexity and whether recessed panels, brackets, or modillions have been added. Let's discuss some types of decoration found on the cornices of American Victorian buildings.

Bracketed Cornices

The most common decoration found on American Victorian structures built of wood is the cornice bracket, which is particularly characteristic of the Italianate Revival style (see Plate 52). Brackets project from the wall or frieze below the cornice and appear to support the roof by attaching to the underside (soffit) of the cornice or eaves of the roof. These brackets are also the Victorian details most often painted incorrectly. There is a tendency today to paint the entire bracket a different color from that used on the frieze and cornice soffit. This was rarely done in the nineteenth century unless decorative moldings linked the brackets together; this was necessary to keep them from appearing to float free of the surrounding structure (see Plates 73, 115, and "The Modillion Cornice" on page 69). Brackets need to be perceived as part of the structural system of buildings of traditional design. In particular, Italianate buildings with deep, overhanging cornices, or mansard-roofed buildings where the roof is so prominent a feature, need brackets to provide an appearance of support; they seem to hold up the roof. This sense of structure is lost if the brackets are isolated from their surrounding elements. *Consequently, brackets should be painted the same color as the frieze and cornice, usually the principal trim color.*

By the mid-nineteenth century most brackets were not cut by the carpenter on the job—contrary to popular myth, as perpetuated by expressions such as "Carpenter Gothic" or "Carpenter Vernacular" so often applied to American frame houses of the second half of the century. Instead, the local builder or lumberyard usually purchased brackets from the catalogues of large steam-planing mills that mass-produced building elements and

PLATE 68. *A mid-nineteenth-century Italianate house shown in Fawn stucco with Old Gold wooden trimmings. Note in particular how the panels of the frieze have been picked out with the body color against the trim color. Normally the recessed edges of the sandwich brackets would also be shown picked out.* The Painter *(April 1885).* The Athenaeum of Philadelphia Collection

PLATE 69. *A mansard-roofed house costing $2,800 to build in the 1880s emphasizes the importance of painting all vertical and horizontal trim elements that suggest structure. Here the strength of the upward thrust from the foundation to the cornice brackets—which appear to support the roof— is intensified by the Medium Brownstone trim against the Light Brownstone body. The trim color also enhances the brackets and recessed panels of the cornice against a soffit and frieze painted in the body color. John Lucas & Co., Portfolio of Modern House Painting Designs (Philadelphia, 1887).* The Athenaeum of Philadelphia Collection

PLATE 70. *A variety of prefabricated brackets of a type available from planing mills after the Civil War. Most of these would qualify for sandwich-bracket picking out.* Foster-Munger Company, Doors, Blinds, Glazed Sash, Mouldings . . . *(Chicago, 1892).* The Athenaeum of Philadelphia Collection

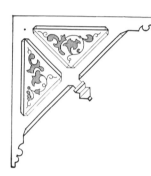

PLATE 71. *A typical Stick-style bracket that is often found painted in two colors. The bracket itself would carry the trim color to match the surrounding woodwork, while the carved recessed panels are picked out in the body color. Chamfered edges may be picked out in red.* Foster-Munger Company, Doors, Blinds, Glazed Sash, Mouldings . . . *(Chicago, 1892).* The Athenaeum of Philadelphia Collection

PLATE 73. *Raking modillion cornice with blocks picked out but visually linked together by the band of quarter-round molding.*

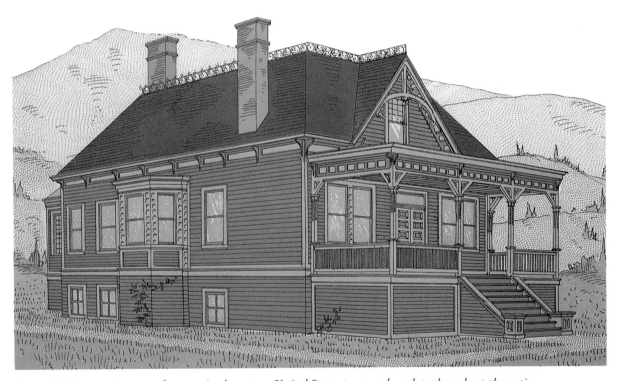

PLATE 74. *Large paint manufacturers in the eastern United States penetrated markets throughout the nation in the 1880s; California, in particular, felt their influence. This cottage, according to John Lucas & Co. of Philadelphia, is "a general favorite on the Western coast of the United States, especially in California, where many of them may be seen with their artistic gables, bay windows and porches, entwined with roses and other creeping vines, relieved against the luxuriant verdure of the picturesque landscape." As is appropriate for a simple house, only a single body color—in this case Straw—and a single trim color—here Medium Brownstone—are used. The cornice brackets are painted in the body color, and the trim color is introduced into the recessed panels of the cornice on both the main body of the house and the porch. John Lucas & Co.,* Portfolio of Modern House Painting Designs *(Philadelphia, 1887).* The Athenaeum of Philadelphia Collection

PLATE 72. *A shockingly overgrown Pennsylvania farmhouse photographed by the United States View Company of Richfield, Pennsylvania, at the end of the nineteenth century. The light body color is fully picked out with a darker trim, especially the sandwich brackets and the moldings of the cornice and frieze of the main roof and bays. This paint scheme also departs from the usual Victorian practice by having light-colored sash rather than the more usual dark sash.* Photograph courtesy of Jay Ruby from an original print in the collection of Mrs. Martha Graybill

PLATE 75. *Some decorative brackets have raised elements that may be picked out in the body color against the trim color.*

PLATE 76. *Modillion cornice of a modest mansard-roofed house with a detail of the continuous band of quarter-round molding painted the body color.*

shipped them by rail throughout the region. After the Civil War virtually all areas of the country were supplied with preprinted trade catalogues such as the "Universal moulding book, containing sections (full size) of mouldings in great variety, architraves, stair and pew railings, brackets, pickets, lattice, scroll work, balusters, newel posts, etc., front and inside doors, folding and sliding doors, store doors, elevation of door and window frames, pew ends, wood mantels, working plans, etc." Catalogues such as this one were distributed by planing mills to the local lumberyards or contractors who in turn stamped them with their own names and addresses. In this fashion the large steam-planing mills unwittingly homogenized the architectural details of an entire area, just as the ready-mixed paint companies gradually eliminated regional differences in color use.[23]

Some of these prefabricated brackets are cookie-cutter simple, consisting of a flat plank of two-inch-thick pine cut to a pattern with a band saw. These inexpensive elements were applied to countless thousands of American buildings as visual fillers on roof cornices or between porch posts, and they were intended to be painted the color of the surrounding elements. In their treatment of brackets, modern painters often reveal their misunderstanding of Victorian exterior decoration: having painted the brackets in the trim color they are unable to leave well enough alone and proceed to paint the leading edge of each bracket a different color, too often bright scarlet. A close examination of nineteenth-century photographs as well as examination of surviving structures reveals that simple brackets were rarely picked out in this fashion.

That was not the case, however, with the more expensive brackets composed of several layers of wood sandwiched together. "Sandwich brackets" come in an

PLATE 77. *A Colonial Revival design with modillioned cornice of a type found in many parts of America at the end of the nineteenth century, shown with a deep Sylvan Green body, Ivory trim, and Victoria Red roof. Alternative schemes suggested by the manufacturer include warm gray trimmed with ivory and a green roof; a Terra Cotta body trimmed with ivory and a deep green roof; Light Olive body and "flesh"-colored trim with a red roof. Acme White Lead and Color Works (Detroit, c. 1895).* The Athenaeum of Philadelphia Collection

endless variety of patterns but usually consist of two decoratively band-sawed boards applied on either side of a third (see Plate 70). The painting of these brackets is simple to master. Think of them as a cheese sandwich on rye. The two decoratively cut elements (the slices of bread) are painted to match the cornice and frieze, but the center (the cheese) is painted another color, either the body color of a clapboard house or a lighter or darker shade of the trim color on a masonry structure. (However, if the cornice is painted a stone color and sanded to simulate stone, there should be *no* picking out.) Usually the "cheese" will be recessed from the leading edges of the "bread" or will contain decorative elements that may project slightly. The picking out calls attention to these decorations without destroying the structural relationship between the brackets and the cornice.

The Modillion Cornice

Nineteenth-century structures, particularly those with detailing inspired more by classical than by Italianate architecture, often have modillions. These horizontal

brackets or consoles may be in the shape of a scroll with an acanthus leaf, but on most vernacular American buildings are simple rectangular blocks (see Plate 77). You should paint modillions the same trim color as the cornice of which they are a part; it is best not to pick out the modillions in the body color against the trim. Modillions relate visually to the structural system and painting them another color makes them appear to float without relationship to the surrounding elements. Worse yet, when a cornice follows the rake of a front-facing gable or large dormer roof line, picking out the block modillions—or smaller blocks, called *dentils*—gives the building an unpleasant bared-tooth grin worthy of a great white shark.

Nearly every generalization has its exceptions. Nineteenth-century photographs occasionally reveal modillions picked out in the body color. But close examination will also reveal that the blocks are tied into the cornice by a continuous band of quarter-round molding painted the body color (see Plate 73). There is also an exception to the generalization that the fascia and soffit are painted in the trim color. According to the manufacturers of Breinig's Ready Mixed Paints, "Where the body color

PLATE 78. *Handsome example of a historical paint scheme on a cottage. The effect was nearly spoiled, however, by the picking out of individual dentils like teeth.*

is lighter than the trimming color, use *both* colors on the cornice, placing the body color on the underside of the cornice [the soffit] and painting the mouldings and frieze with the darker color." This technique, illustrated in Plate 72, has the effect of breaking up what otherwise might be a massive band of dark trim directly under the roof. This lighter band of color also reflects light and heightens the shadows cast by decorative elements such as brackets or modillions.[24]

FRIEZE PANELS

Below the cornice the frieze of an entablature may also be decorated with panels and moldings (see Plates 68 and 79). On masonry structures with wooden cornices painted in a stone color and sanded to simulate stone— the color of which may have been suggested by some

genuine stone used elsewhere on the structure—you should not pick out the panels or moldings with another color; the shadows cast by the moldings will provide adequate emphasis. On wooden frame structures, however, you can introduce the body color into the panels or onto the moldings of the frieze; this is an acceptable historical painting technique.

CORNERS

Once the principle of outlining with the trim color is grasped, it comes as no surprise that those elements of the trim that define the corners of buildings also require special attention. Nearly all clapboard and quite a few masonry structures erected in the nineteenth century will have one of three types of corner treatment: corner boards, pilasters, or quoins.

PLATE 79. *These two examples show color schemes for simple houses in the 1880s. The one on the left has a body painted in Medium Olive trimmed in Medium Brownstone with Reddish Brown sash. The other house has two body colors—Medium Brownstone and Terra Cotta—and two values of Olive for trim. Note the picking out of the frieze panels on the mansardic house, and the way the decorative detail on the bottom of the vertical board siding is highlighted by the trim color on the house on the right. Rossiter & Wright,* Modern House Painting *(1883).* The Athenaeum of Philadelphia Collection

PLATE 80. *This nineteenth-century photograph of a well-picked-out mansard-roofed house in Vermont confirms several details of historical painting—particularly the frieze panels, sandwich brackets, porch posts, bay window, and under-porch grill.* Photograph courtesy of the Society for the Preservation of New England Antiquities

PLATE 82. *Inspired by the Swiss style, this house in northern New Jersey relies on the careful placement of the trim color to bring out its attractive detailing—as suggested in Plate 79.*

PLATE 81. *"The building represented in this plate was designed for Summer use at one of our seaside watering resorts. It is, however, just as it is shown . . . , admirably adapted for street use in most of the picturesque little cities and towns of California. Its exterior form and ornamentation is of the Swiss style, although the stories are higher than are generally used in Swiss buildings. The almost excessive frill work gives it a very pretty, although a rather tawdry appearance."* The temptation today would be to adopt a Boutique approach to emphasize different textures; yet the house is shown in only two body colors: as is usual, the darker—in this case, Dark Olive—is on the first floor: the lighter—Terra Cotta—is on the shingled second floor. A third color—Old Gold—is used for all the trim except the roof cresting. Notice that the exuberant trim is not picked out; its light color against the darker body provides adequate definition. The first-floor body and trim color are reversed on the doors, step-base moldings, panels, risers, posts, and the porch latticework. *Seeley Bros. Paint Company (New York, 1886).* Collection of Mr. and Mrs. Lewis Seeley, The Athenaeum of Philadelphia

PLATE 83. *This Stick-style gable carries a third color, which calls attention to the decorative siding. (Note the improper shutter mounting.)*

Corner Boards

Corner boards are applied to the external corners of clapboard buildings to provide a surface against which the cut ends of the siding are fitted. Visually, they carry the sense of structure from the cornice to the foundation. Consequently, corner boards must be picked out with the same trim color as all the horizontal elements: water table, belt course, and cornice. Corner boards also appear on towers and at joints where the clapboards change direction around bays or additions. *It is essential that all of these vertical boards be uniformly painted in the trim color to provide the structural definition required by historical paint schemes* (see Plates 84 and 85).

Pilasters

Pilasters are attached—the architectural term is *engaged*—piers or pillars that project slightly from the wall of a building and often have a classical capital and base

(see Plate 35). They are found in a simplified form on nearly all Greek Revival buildings of the early nineteenth century (usually painted white) and occasionally on both residential and commercial Colonial Revival structures of the later nineteenth or early twentieth century. You should treat pilasters in the same way as corner boards and paint them in the main trim color for the same reasons. Pilasters, especially when they appear in lieu of corner boards, may have recessed panels that may be echoed by panels in the frieze below the cornice. In these cases, you can paint the recesses on both frieze and pilasters in the body color to good effect. One note of warning: If the pilasters are fluted like classical columns do not attempt to pick out each semicircular or semielliptical flute unless you intend to create a "painted lady." On masonry structures, you can paint the wooden pilasters in a trim color selected to simulate stone, perhaps even "sanded" to heighten the illusion. In such cases, do not pick out recesses in the pilasters or frieze with another color.

Quoins

Quoins are those blocks of brick or stone—or wood cut to imitate masonry—found on the external corners of a wall (see Plate 87). They accentuate different surface treatments or materials and define the corners of buildings. You are most likely to encounter quoins when repainting stucco or brick structures that originally were not painted. In these cases, you would do best to copy the color of any unpainted stone trim on the house or simulate a stone color (see discussion under "Sanded Paint" on pages 57–63). Needless to say, unpainted stone or brick quoins should not be painted if they have escaped being coated for the past century! On clapboard structures with quoins cut to imitate stone, you can heighten the simulation by painting the quoins the trim color, as one might the corner boards of an ordinary clapboard house. As a general rule, you should choose for such buildings color schemes that utilize stone colors.

FOUNDATIONS

Just as the roof is often forgotten when a paint scheme is being planned, the areas of the house at foundation level may also be overlooked. Victorian architects and builders intended foundations to be seen, not obscured by shrubbery. One suspects that the coarse and rapidly growing evergreens sold as "foundation plantings" are favored by suburban developers because they disguise the ugly concrete-block foundations of modern tract houses. But like Great Dane puppies, those plantings continue to grow. The Victorians correctly believed that

PLATE 84. *It was rather unusual for a paint company to publish a flank elevation rather than the main façade. For that reason, this plate and Plate 85 are useful to illustrate the picking out of Shingle-style and Queen Anne–style houses. Here the body has been painted Fawn and the trim Dark Brownstone. Heath & Milligan Manufacturing Company,* Best Prepared Paints for Ready Use *(Chicago, c. 1890).* The Athenaeum of Philadelphia Collection

PLATE 85. *Flank elevation of a Queen Anne style illustrating picking out in Dark Olive Green against a Light Olive Green body. Heath & Milligan Manufacturing Company,* Best Prepared Paints for Ready Use *(Chicago, c. 1890).* The Athenaeum of Philadelphia Collection

PLATE 86. *The Cape Island Presbyterian Church (1853; now a community center) in Cape May, New Jersey, with its exotic Moorish tower, is otherwise a late Neoclassical structure. The pilasters are painted the trim color and then accentuated by picking out the recesses in the body color.*

PLATE 87. *No building was safe from the colorful Victorians. Shown here is the most famous Philadelphia country house, Mount Pleasant (1763), with a Light Drab body and Light Brownstone trim. Originally the stucco had been pale yellow and the quoins unpainted brick. "Town and Country Ready Mixed Paints," Harrison Bros. & Co., c. 1884.* Collection of Mr. and Mrs. Edward D. Dart, The Athenaeum of Philadelphia

such vegetation, especially when allowed to flourish unchecked, harbored insects and held moisture close to the house, causing paint failure, mildew, and unhealthy interior humidity. The mid-nineteenth-century British landscape gardener Edward Kemp argued that "in the immediate neighbourhood of the house . . . it is particularly desirable that trees and shrubs should not abound. Independently of darkening the windows, they communicate great dampness to the walls, and prevent that action of the wind upon the building which alone can keep it dry, comfortable, and consequently healthy." In addition, planting close to the foundation "prevents the true proportions, outlines, and details of a building from being properly seen and rightly appreciated." Despite the climatic differences between the British Isles and North America, Frank Jesup Scott quoted Kemp in his own *Art of Beautifying Suburban Home Grounds* and added that American physicians "attribute much of the consumption so fatal in New England families, to the want of sun, the damp air, and the tree and shrub-embowered and shutter-closed houses peculiar to its villages and farms."[25]

Victorian stone and brick foundations, therefore, were more often than not visible; houses rose directly from the well-tended lawns shown in thousands of nineteenth-century prints and photographs (see Plates 2, 8, and 29). If left to grow unchecked, plants such as yews gradually blur the definition between lawn and house, making the building appear to float above a ragged band of green. If you seek an authentic exterior appearance for your house, you should consider removing most foundation plantings. This may seem a draconian measure, especially if your plants are treasured varieties. Fortunately, many of these plants can be saved by being moved to other locations away from the house. However, do check first to see if a healthy, well-rounded specimen of the same variety cannot be purchased from a nursery and planted for approximately the same cost; the prudent decision may be to sacrifice the plants.

While Victorians did not obscure the foundations with shrubbery, they did accent the foundations with *corner* planting. For such accent points most landscape gardeners suggested materials like Rose of Sharon and forsythia kept well under control.

Once overgrown plants have been cut away, and their roots thoroughly grubbed from the soil around foundations and porches, the surface should be regraded. Be sure to create a slope that pitches away from the house; this should be done before replanting is begun. Healthy sod can then be brought in and low bedding plants or ground cover set out. Appropriate plants for close to the house are salvias, geraniums, dahlias, verbenas, or ferns—all create low beds that rarely reach above the water table of a typical residential Victorian building.[26]

If your house has no gutters and downspouts, you might create a drip line of pebbles 24 to 36 inches wide where the water falls from the eaves around the foundation. This looks crisp, prevents mud splashes on the

PLATE 88. *The house on the left shows vestigial quoins picked out on a successful gray-and-white Boutique treatment in San Francisco. Illustrated below is the Second Empire–style, mansard-roofed residence of Mr. Charles K. Partridge, Augusta, Maine, as painted and reproduced by the Atlas Ready-Mixed Paint Company, Philadelphia, c. 1890. The body is Fawn or Straw and the quoins, painted Medium Brownstone, accentuate and define the corners of the house. The porch and window trim are painted Medium Olive, while the sash is Indian Red.* The Athenaeum of Philadelphia Collection

brick of the foundation, and covers the terra cotta sewer tiles that carry the rainwater to a dry well or storm sewer. More than one damp basement has been cured by regrading soil around the foundation and burying a line of drainpipe to carry roof runoff (see Plate 89).

When Victorian foundations are newly exposed, a whole host of hidden problems may appear. (In fact, now that the true condition of the foundation is seen for the first time, you may discover that it requires repairs beyond the scope of this book and the skills of the average homeowner.) You should examine the pointing and have a skilled mason renew it if necessary, using a sand and lime mortar—not Portland cement—matched to the color of the original. You may also discover that the foundation had originally been painted, a dark brick red being the most common color. Rossiter and Wright stated in the 1880s, "Foundations . . . can generally be left to take care of themselves" in matters of color. "If they are of good stone they should not be touched, and if they are in brick, the best thing to do is to give the bricks two coats of oil with perhaps a red stain." Even if the foundation shows no sign of originally having been painted, you may decide that such a treatment is an attractive alternative to more expensive repairs if the brick (or a stuccoed surface) has been irregularly patched or poorly repointed over the years. Take care that the surface is clean and dry before you begin painting; scrape the soil away from the foundation, wire-brush the surface, flush well with clean water, and allow to dry thoroughly before painting using oil-base paint. Foundation colors are always dark; the fastest way known to spoil a paint scheme is to paint the foundation a bright color, especially sky-blue.[27]

WATER TABLE

One of the most commonly missed details of exterior decoration is the water table, which is often obscured by overgrown and inappropriate plantings. This trim may be nothing more than a simple board below the siding of clapboard buildings, and you should paint it in the overall trim color to match the corner boards and cornice. The water table usually joins with the fascia of the porch deck trim to continue the horizontal outline above the foundation (see Plate 90).

UNDER-PORCH GRILLS AND LATTICEWORK

Most Victorian porches are elevated on brick or stone piers or wooden posts and the spaces between are filled with latticework or decoratively pierced solid boards (see Plate 90). These under-porch grills or latticework

PLATE 89. *A crushed-stone drip line creates a neat transition between lawn and foundation, prevents mud splashes, and hides terra cotta drains.* Photograph by George B. Tatum.

PLATE 90. *A porch detail of the house shown in Plate 76 illustrates picking out of the water table, porch posts, balusters, and grill.*

visually continue the foundation and allow for the free circulation of air under the porch floor, which discourages moisture from injuring joists and decking. Normally these lattices and grills are held by two- to three-inch-wide beaded or chamfered frames that fit the opening and rest—incorrectly—directly on the ground. Consequently they may rot and must be repaired before painting. You should suspend latticework frames off the ground from the underside of the porch framing or by attaching them to the supporting posts. If that is not practical, you can sink flat stones or bricks into the turf so the restored and newly painted lattice or grill frames do not come in contact with the ground. Another good technique is to remove a few inches of soil under the porch, spread a moisture barrier of plastic sheeting, and then cover the area with three inches of gravel.[28]

The placement of paint on under-porch grills is relatively simple: the frames carry the principal trim color, and the lattice or decoratively pierced panels are painted in the body color. You should apply this practice when the grills are approximately one to three feet in height. Occasionally, however, grills are five to six feet in height, especially on late Queen Anne structures with high foundations and wraparound porches. In these instances you may need to paint the grill in a single dark trim color to provide a sense of foundation for the porch. For the latticework under the porches of masonry buildings, you should use paint of the masonry color or a lighter or darker value of the trim color to provide some contrast.

WINDOW GRILLS

Basement windows or foundation vents, often covered or surrounded by decorative cast iron, are another feature you may uncover by slashing away the jungle of rampant plantings. You should paint window frames and sash following the color scheme already selected for the upper-level windows. Iron grills or decorative vents, however, may be wholly painted in the trim color or treated like other ironwork in a Bronze Green or black. Original iron elements are often rusted or heavily caked with deteriorated paint. They should be removed, cleaned—lightly sandblasted if necessary—primed, reinstalled, and painted (see "Iron Porch Posts," page 83).

WOODEN STEPS

The risers of wooden steps are normally painted the trim color, while the treads carry the porch deck color down to the ground. Recesses or decorative panels on either side of the steps allow you to reintroduce the body color. The handrail and balusters of the steps follow the same rules applied on the porch: top and bottom rails in the trim color and the balusters in the body color. If the porch itself is painted and sanded to simulate stone, you should, of course, treat the steps and rails the same way to match the porch.

If your building has acquired a modern fire escape that cannot be removed, your only choices are to paint it in the trim and deck colors to match the porch treatment, or, if this would make the stairs too apparent, to paint the entire fire escape the main color of the house in an effort to make it disappear. A metal fire escape on a masonry building would probably look best in a dark olive green.

PORCHES

A Victorian porch! Even for a city-bred person, the very words call forth nostalgic images in sepia: crickets and fireflies on Midwestern summer nights . . . heat light-

PLATE 91. *The Victorian porch of summer delights: the Mainstay Inn, Cape May, New Jersey—gray floor and deep-green shutters and furniture.*

ning in the distance . . . familiar greetings from strolling neighbors. And porch swings—always *green* swings suspended below *blue* ceilings above *gray* floors. These swings, and their inevitable companions, the wide-armed green porch rockers, always seem to have had green-and-white-striped awning-canvas cushions filled with horsehair or straw, retrieved each spring from storage in the carriage house to the regret of nesting field mice. So, too, the wicker furniture on porches at seaside houses in our youth came only in white. And shutters! As if by some natural law shutters could only be the deepest green. These colors we now know are long-established conventions, holdovers from an age without air conditioning or television when life appeared to move at a more leisurely pace.

Of course the realities of maintaining a century-old porch are less romantic and all too often written in red. The cost of care and repair of Victorian porches is so great that you would do well to keep yours protected with paint. Since the most characteristic Victorian features of a house may be concentrated on the band-sawed-and-turned elements of the porch, the placement of the colors becomes particularly critical.

PLATE 92. *Sky blue being reapplied to the porch ceiling of a Colonial Revival house of 1890–1900.*

Traditional Paint Colors for Porches

Let's begin with those traditional porch colors: blue for ceilings and gray for floors. Both have survived because they are practical. Designed to protect occupants from the direct effects of sun and rain, porches need reflected light to keep them from being too dark. Blue on porch ceilings may continue the ancient architectural tradition of suggesting the sky overhead; Renaissance decorators even added clouds to heighten that illusion. The gray floor is also practical; it is less likely to show dust and tracks than lighter or darker colors. A dark floor is handsome when recently painted and a scrubbed white floor looks fresh, but the first dusty day followed by a spotting rain will graphically illustrate why the Victorians most often settled on neutral gray.[29]

Occasionally, porch ceilings of boards were stained and varnished. Usually these surfaces subsequently acquired coats of paint, which, failing to bond to the varnish, are now flaking off. Ideally, you should completely remove the later paint, restain the exposed wood, and apply to the clean, dry surface several coats of exterior-grade marine varnish. If that is not feasible, you can simply paint the ceiling in appropriate colors after removing the old finishes.

If the undersides of your porch ceiling rafters are exposed, you might paint using a *combination* of the body and trim colors. Nineteenth-century paint companies commonly suggested the use of the body color on the ceiling as an alternative to blue, and we have occasionally found both body and trim colors used. For example, on a clapboard house painted yellow with brown trim, the ceiling itself (actually the underside of the roof decking) could be painted yellow and the exposed rafters brown. Often the pattern of these rafters is visually interesting—especially if the porch wraps around the building—and picking out calls attention to features that otherwise might pass unnoticed. If the rafter ends project through the cornice of your porch, you should paint them out with the porch trim (in the example above, brown). However, if you give porch ceiling and rafters a two-color treatment you should continue the part of the roof that forms the overhang in the body color so the darker rafter ends are highlighted.

Porch Floors

Floors are among the most vulnerable porch surfaces—they are where paint failure and resulting wood decay are most likely to occur. Before painting, you should make certain all damaged or deteriorated flooring is replaced. Also examine supporting piers and joists to be

PLATE 93. *Porch floor painted in checkerboard pattern simulates blocks of marble at Andalusia—Nicholas Biddle's country house designed by Thomas Ustick Walter in 1833—reproducing a pattern discovered at another Neoclassical house in the Philadelphia area.* Photograph courtesy of James Biddle

Wooden Porch Posts

Simple rectangular wooden posts receive no picking out— you should paint them to match the overall trim of the building as part of the outlining that defines the structure. Sometimes square posts were milled with bevels at the angles to form chamfers. These additional surfaces of one half to a full inch in width often terminate in a decorative "lamb's tongue" flourish. While the chamfers are usually painted the same color as the post, you may also pick them out against the trim color in either the body color or in scarlet (see Plate 94). However, it is better not to overuse such decorative devices. We never recommend that the chamfers be picked out in scarlet except when physical examination of the structure discloses scarlet having been used in the nineteenth century. There seems to be no consistent pattern to suggest when the "scarlet chamfer"—like scarlet putty used in window sash—would have been used; we've discovered it on modest houses and grand villas in locations all across the United States. It is a variable that simply reflects the painter, architect, or owner's taste.

sure there are no hidden problems. Then meticulously prepare the surface (see the Appendix), prime in oil paint, and apply two finish coats.

The traditional color for Victorian porch floors is gray, but we have often used the body or trim color to good effect if one or the other is neither too light nor too dark. The floor need not be painted in one color alone. You can paint the floorboards in alternating colors to create stripes. If the boards are of random width, badly patched, or narrow, chalk lines may be snapped at regular intervals of six to ten inches, and you can paint stripes without regard to actual floorboard width. Another technique especially appropriate to Neoclassical houses is a checkerboard of light and dark blocks simulating masonry that can even be marbleized to heighten the illusion (see Plate 93). As a general rule, you are better off avoiding these decorative porch floor treatments. Stripes on the floor of a simple house or marble blocks on an elevated Stick-style veranda would look silly, and porch floors require regular repainting that should be achieved as easily and inexpensively as possible.

PLATE 94. *The scarlet chamfer used on porch posts at the Queen Victoria Inn, Cape May, New Jersey.*

Our note of caution regarding the overuse of decorative devices such as the scarlet chamfer has some basis in historical criticism. Ehrick Kensett Rossiter and Frank Ayers Wright argued in the 1880s,

> Let it be borne in mind that color is chiefly important in architecture as an adjunct of form, and that it can never quite take the place of form. On the exterior, color can properly emphasize form, but it should never be used so that it interferes with picturesqueness of outline and refined detail. We refer more particularly to the custom of painting chamferings, mouldings and ornamentation in a positive color—frequently a bright red. These features in a design ought to be appreciated in light and shade only. They bring out the form in detail, and the emphasis of shadow is quite good enough without recourse to more violent methods.

As with the persistence of critics' complaints about all-white houses trimmed in green, picking out of ornamentation in positive colors must have been fairly widespread to cause this comment. Even the paint companies occasionally exhibited the practice (see Plate 2).[30]

Some porch posts are partially round. These also are painted in the trim color, but you may pick out the turned rings or clusters of rings with the body color or with red, or you may even gild them. According to the manufacturer of Breinig's Ready Mixed Paints (c. 1886), "where the body color is lighter than the trimming color . . . , the dark color should be applied to the rails and square parts of the posts, filling in the turned work with a lighter color." This technique clearly has been used on the house shown in Plate 95. Not everyone was in agreement on this picking out of turned elements, however, especially after painting schemes became simpler in the early twentieth century. In a 1914 essay entitled "How to Make Your Home Attractive," the Lowe Brothers Company of Dayton, Ohio, argued, "The main thing to avoid in house painting is patchiness. Treat the house as a unit, subduing any ornaments and useless bric-a-brac by the color scheme. In general all portions of one idea should be in one color or tone. For instance in the case of a porch post or column do not paint the base and cap one color and the shaft another. From start to finish it is a column and should be treated as such. In fact the whole porch is one idea and generally should be treated in one color."[31]

Iron Porch Posts

Cast-iron veranda or porch posts that survive in large numbers in cities such as New Orleans and Savannah were commonly used in many parts of the United States

PLATE 95. *This otherwise modest village house in Pennsylvania at the end of the nineteenth century has been picked out, probably by applying the body color to the recessed panels of the frieze, porch brackets, and turned parts of the porch posts. Wooden plank sidewalks were common in lumbering areas of America.* Photograph courtesy of Jay Ruby from an original United States View Company print in the collection of Mrs. Martha Graybill

PLATE 96. *Exuberant picking out of the porch posts and balustrade of the Queen Anne–style Fitzgerald House, Cortland, New York (see Plate 29).*

in the mid-nineteenth century. Relatively cheap to manufacture, but difficult to deliver because of their weight, iron verandas similar to the ones illustrated in Plates 51 and 97 could be acquired by anyone who lived in a location serviced by a river, canal, or railroad. Much of the famous pre–Civil War New Orleans ironwork, for example, carries the label of manufacturers such as Wood and Perrot in Philadelphia or Hutchinson and Wickersham in New York. The latter firm waxed lyrical in 1857 over its product:

> Verandahs are portions of a country house which cannot be dispensed with, nor are they to be overlooked in preparing plans for City and Suburban residences. In one of these delightful shelters, there is a sense of enjoyment to be found that can be had nowhere else. In a Country-seat especially are they needed. Through them comes the view of pleasant twilights, and the evening breezes blow sweetly among the climbing plants that cover them. Walls are hot, and fresh air is what is wanted under all circumstances. The Iron Verandah offers advantages which no other material can

possibly furnish. Its graceful and open fabric lends ornament to the dwelling, it permits a consultation of all tastes, it impedes no current of air, and it is at once substantial and elegant.[32]

While it is common today to find cast-iron veranda posts, railings, and friezes painted black, the most popular color in the nineteenth century was the shade of Bronze Green so often recommended for roofs and sometimes for shutters. Black became common over the years as homeowners told their painters to "match existing colors." Each time the iron was painted the painter added slightly more black as he mixed the green; ultimately the shade was so dark that it was simpler to apply black. The return to green for veranda ironwork, especially if the roof is to be painted in stripes, is a subtle and satisfying change. Green appears to have been used regardless of the colors selected for the trim and siding colors.[33]

As the Wickersham advertising copy suggests, the romantic imagery that is such a part of modern nostalgia for nineteenth-century architecture has Victorian roots. What could be more evocative than a cast-iron veranda painted a deep Bronze Green and twined with wisteria hung with showy clusters of bluish, white, pink, or purplish flowers? Alas, these woody vines with soft tendrils insinuate themselves into small gaps in the ironwork pattern and cunningly weave in and out as they reach upward toward the sun. Each year the coils grow larger and stronger, gradually swelling to fill the gaps, forcing apart weak joints and rupturing fragile patterns. Romantic or not, aggressive vines such as wisteria should not be permitted to establish themselves on veranda

PLATE 97. *Cast-iron veranda by the New York firm of Hutchinson and Wickersham as reproduced from its catalogue of 1857. Notice that the metal tent roof was clearly intended to be striped.* The Athenaeum of Philadelphia Collection

PLATE 98. *Dark Blue Green has been used to good effect on the ironwork of the recently repainted Romanesque Revival McDonnell-Pierce House (1858) in Madison, Wisconsin, now operated as the Mansion Hill Inn. The wooden trim is Light Drab to match the cut sandstone body, and the sash is Indian Red.* Photograph by Zane Williams, courtesy of the Alexander Company

posts. If you want to have such plants, be sure to keep them well trimmed by removing the heavy, woody branches every few years—or better yet, erect a small framework of green pipe on which the vines can be trained.

Balustrades

Consider the typical Victorian balustrade. It may be found around the edge of a grand balcony or between the posts of a modest porch. It comes in an almost infinite variety of forms. Yet it usually consists of two parallel rails held in place by pedestals, or porch posts with the space between occupied by balusters that may be decoratively scrolled, square, or turned. Keeping in mind that the porch *posts* are normally painted the trim color, it should come as no surprise that both the rails are also painted the trim color. This treatment helps to continue the outlining that is typical of historical house painting.

What then should you do with the balusters? Look at

Plates 99, 100, and 101; in all of these examples the balusters are painted a different color, usually lighter, than the rails. In fact, we know from physical examination of surviving structures that wooden balusters are usually painted the principal body color of the house, as is shown in Plates 99 and 101. Even when a house is painted only two colors, the principal body color is usually reintroduced on the balusters to fill in the space defined by the rails and porch posts.

Porch Furniture

Wooden porch furniture was usually painted dark green. An elderly painter once told us that porch swings, rockers, and plant stands were always painted a green that he obtained by mixing equal parts of Kelly green and black. Examination of porch furniture that has been stored for generations, recollections of the elderly, and microanalysis of the furniture surfaces confirms this long tradition. The exception appears to be wicker furniture, which often was painted white.

PLATE 99. *As a general rule, the less complex the trimmings of a house, the fewer colors used. Here body and trim colors have been reversed to enliven an otherwise plain farm house where the introduction of an additional color would not have been appropriate. On the porches, the recessed panels of the doors, the brackets, the soffit of the cornice, the moldings of the posts, and the flat balusters of the railing have been picked out in the body color against the trim color. The trim color has also been used on the crown molding of the brick chimney caps and to outline the panel molding below the porches. Seeley Bros.* (c. 1880) The Athenaeum of Philadelphia Collection

PLATE 100. *Perhaps captured by the photographer while discussing overdue fence repairs, this rural Pennsylvania couple stands before their vernacular house that appears painted in two colors—body and trim—which have been reversed to pick out the few decorative features.* Photograph courtesy of Jay Ruby from an original print in the collection of Mrs. Martha Graybill

PLATE 101. *A late-nineteenth-century photograph by Edwin N. Peabody of Salem, Massachusetts, illustrates the picking out of a simple cottage with sawed balusters.* Photograph courtesy of the Society for the Preservation of New England Antiquities

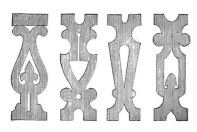

PLATE 102. *Simple balusters of the type that could be cut by local carpenters but, after the Civil War, were increasingly ordered from catalogues of steam-planing mills.* Foster-Munger Company, Doors, Blinds, Glazed Sash, Mouldings . . . *(Chicago, 1892).* The Athenaeum of Philadelphia Collection

PLATE 103. *An emphatic structural sense common to Stick-style buildings is given to the E. B. Burton residence in Manchester, Vermont, by the placement of the trim color. Notice how the porch cornice and posts and the gable cornices have been picked out, probably with the body color. The jig-sawed baluster fence is particularly interesting and is probably painted in the body and trim colors of the house. Alternatively, the fence would probably be green.* Photograph courtesy of the Society for the Preservation of New England Antiquities

PLATE 104. *According to F. W. Devoe & Company, "The style of house here represented is very prevalent and deservedly popular in all parts of the country. It is economical as far as cost of construction is concerned, spacious and commodious, and when treated with due regard to taste in decoration is capable of making an excellent appearance." Quite often Stick-style porches such as this one on an otherwise vernacular house are painted a single trim color without the picking out that is typical of turned baluster porches of the same period. Notice the intentional difference in roller-blind colors between the upper and lower stories.* Exterior Decoration *(New York: F. W. Devoe & Company, 1885), plate IX.* Dornsife Collection of the Victorian Society in America at The Athenaeum of Philadelphia

PLATE 105. *The ultimate in fashionable exterior decoration in Norwich, Connecticut, late in the nineteenth century. Note color placement on porches and bays as well as the strong vertical and horizontal lines of the typical Stick-style framing.* Photograph courtesy of the Society for the Preservation of New England Antiquities

WINDOWS

Throughout the discussion of color placement for wooden residential buildings, we've stressed the importance of *outlining* the structure to define the mass of the building. Now we begin introducing another dimension by calling attention to the shadows and highlights that give character to all Victorian buildings. By the thoughtful choice and placement of color it is possible to cause some elements to *project* toward and others to *recede* from our view as we gaze at your building. One paint company used these terms in a promotional flyer published in 1885 when the taste for multicolor paint schemes was at its height, "Where it is desired to bring out or fully preserve the structural design, the projecting parts, called high lights, should be lighter in color than the receding or sunken parts, called shadows."[34]

The introduction of Queen Anne, Shingle, and Stick-style buildings in the later decades of the nineteenth century encouraged these treatments. The author of *Ex-terior Decoration, A Treatise on the Artistic Use of Colors in the Ornamentation of Buildings*, produced in 1885 by F. W. Devoe & Company, pointed out that "the many fronts, diversified as to material, with visible framing, shingle or smooth covering, the gables, the porches, etc., all provide a means for the employment of parti-colored effects, the most attractive and artistically valuable feature of modern house painting, and one that the old box-pattern house, with its plain flat front, does not so readily admit of."[35]

It is the loss of the articulation of shadows and highlights that makes monochromatic paint schemes so unsatisfactory for Victorian buildings. As early as the mid-nineteenth century Andrew Jackson Downing argued, "There are features, such as window facings . . . which confer the same kind of expression on a house that the eyes, eyebrows, lips, etc., of a face, do upon the human countenance. To paint the whole house plain drab, gives it very much the same dull and insipid effect that col-ourless features . . . do the face." To avoid this monot-ony, he advocated "painting the bolder projecting features a different shade." If the body of the house is to be painted a light color, Downing recommended that "the facings of the windows, cornices, etc., be painted several shades darker, of the same colour." If the body of the house is dark, "then let the window dressings, etc., be painted of a much lighter shade of the same colour."[36]

While the treatment and colors that Downing recommends would be most appropriate for a building of the mid-nineteenth century, the principle of picking out certain elements—the windows and doors in particular—with a trim color that is lighter or darker than the body of the house remained the rule for most architects and critics until the taste for monochromatic paint schemes returned in the twentieth century. Usually this meant that the "sunken" elements of a building—those voids that receded into the shadows from the main surface of the building—would be *darker* than the surrounding trim or body color. Calvert Vaux reminds us that "the effect of a glass window or opening in a wall is always dark when seen from a distance."[37] Reduced to a practical rule, the sash of most Victorian buildings should be painted the same color as the window frames or darker

than the frames, the latter treatment being most often recommended by nineteenth-century architects and paint manufacturers for wooden residential structures. This rule is not as imprecise as it may appear; the age, style, and material of a building help to determine how sash and window frames are to be painted.

Mid-nineteenth-century residential structures—regardless of material—and virtually all masonry structures, whether residential, commercial, or institutional, are usually painted so the window frames and sash are the same color. However, virtually all wooden residential structures erected after 1876 (with the notable exception of Colonial Revival houses that normally have white or monochromatic window frames and sash) are usually painted so that there is differentiation between the window frames and sash. The frames will usually be painted the trim color to match the cornice, porch, corner boards, etc., but the sash will be even darker—usually deep reddish or chocolate brown, dark green, olive, or even black (see Plates 15 and 32). This creates a sense of the windows receding into the façade, which is exactly the effect that was intended. Not only would

PLATE 106. *By the 1880s American paint companies were recommending several colors for picking out the details of Queen Anne houses. Five colors are specified for this window in the October 1885 issue of* The Painter, *including Old Gold and two shades of Brownstone. The Athenaeum of Philadelphia Collection*

PLATE 107. *This window detail of a Shingle-style house appeared as the frontispiece of the December 1886 issue of* House Painting and Decorating *magazine. The colors include Amber, Light Olive, and two shades of Brownstone. The Athenaeum of Philadelphia Collection*

PLATE 108. *A mid-nineteenth-century Italianate Revival house shown in a simple paint scheme of one color each for body, trim, sash, and shutters. Houses of this type are rarely painted in more than four colors. Here the body is Buff and the trim is Medium Drab or Light Olive. The earth and stone colors recommended by Downing continued to be used throughout the century. The sash is Reddish Brown and the shutters are painted Shutter Green, a color also used on the lattice under the porch.* Exterior Decoration *(New York: F. W. Devoe & Company, 1885), plate III.* Dornsife Collection of the Victorian Society in America at The Athenaeum of Philadelphia

sash painted a lighter color than window frames minimize the sense of shadow, but it would call attention to the muntins (the glazing bars that hold the panes of glass into the sash) and make the windows appear smaller. Throughout the nineteenth century the trend was toward ever-larger panes of glass separated by muntins that were as thin as possible, except when an "antique" effect was intended, as in the small panes occasionally found in the upper sash of Queen Anne houses from the last quarter of the century (Plate 32).

What about post-1876 residential and commercial structures built of masonry? The majority of these should have window frames and sash painted the same color. However, we have found exceptions to this rule, and on several occasions we have specified darker sash on brick or stone houses and commercial structures where a physical examination indicated a similar treatment was

used in the nineteenth century or where the modern owner sought to enlarge the windows visually.

The properly painted window units of a post-Centennial wooden house will probably have frames of the main trim color, which will generally be darker than the body color. The sash will be painted the same color or an even darker one, typically deep reddish brown or blackish green. As early as 1848, C. N. Elliott directed that "sash should be black, or nearly so." According to Sherwin-Williams in 1884, "Sash . . . should be painted very dark. Black or bronze green are good colors for general work. For olive combinations, a dark rich wine color is good for sash. Vandyke brown is the best general color for sash, as it is a warm color, besides being dark, and it harmonizes perfectly with all warm colors." Finally, on high Victorian structures with large panes of glass, the thin line of *putty* that secures each pane may

PLATE 109. *A clapboard Colonial Revival house with vaguely post-Colonial classical forms of c. 1895 shown with a Light Olive body, Moss green trim, and a red roof. Sash and window frames are the same color. Alternative paint schemes suggested by the manufacturer include a Bronze Green body, white trim, and red roof; a lead-color body, white trim, and red roof; a lavender body, ivory trim, and red roof; and a terra cotta body, trimmed in ivory with a deep green roof. Acme White Lead and Color Works (Detroit, c. 1895).* The Athenaeum of Philadelphia Collection

PLATE 111. *The importance of dark sash even for pale Boutique color schemes is well illustrated on this elegant San Francisco house (left). On the house shown below, the sash is Indian Red, as would be expected on a building of the Queen Anne style. The body is two shades of Terra Cotta, the gable Terra Cotta and Amber, and the entire building trimmed in Dark Brownstone.* The Painter *(April 1886).* The Athenaeum of Philadelphia Collection

PLATE 110. *This late Victorian clapboard-and-shingle-sided house is shown with a red roof, deep-green lower body, lead-color upper body, light Straw trimmings, and matching window frames and sash. Alternative suggestions by the manufacturer include green first floor, Light Olive second floor, and white trim; both floors light Straw trimmed in white (with a green roof); Light Olive body with Old Gold trim (green roof); deep-green body and white trim (terra cotta roof); deep-green first floor, Light Olive second floor, and white trim with a red roof.* Acme White Lead and Color Works *(Detroit, c. 1895).* The Athenaeum of Philadelphia Collection

PLATE 112. *Storm windows should always be the same color as the sash. Some manufacturers of aluminum storm and screen units now offer acceptable darker colors—Reddish Brown is the easiest to obtain.*

PLATE 113. *Changing the sash color often requires careful scraping to remove accumulations of paint that have lapped onto the glass.*

be painted the same scarlet used on porch post chamfers. The resulting fine red outline around the glass would not be obvious from any distance, yet it enlivens the overall effect of the completed color scheme. Occasionally several colors may be introduced onto the highly carved window units of Queen Anne houses—see Plate 106—but these are rare, and it is generally safer on simpler windows to confine the painting to trim and sash colors.[38]

Storm windows must be the same color as the sash. This will mean that on most Victorian buildings aluminum storm window units in white or natural metal are unacceptable. Fortunately, it is now possible to acquire aluminum storm windows in several colors, including a dark reddish brown that is nearly perfect for use with sash of that color (Plate 112). Otherwise, it is possible to treat white aluminum so that it will accept an oil-base paint in the color adopted for the sash.

One final note about painting sash. Nine times out of ten, you will be applying the dark color over several coats of white paint that may have invaded the glass by as much as a quarter of an inch around each pane. You will need to scrape away this band of white before or after the dark color is applied. This is a tedious job at best, but like polishing the brass hardware of the front door it is essential to set off a successful paint job.

SHUTTERS

Shutters—or blinds as they were occasionally called—are probably the most misunderstood elements on the exterior of American Victorian buildings. Thought of today as optional ornaments, shutters were essential in the nineteenth century for protection against what the Philadelphia-based architect Samuel Sloan called "light-footed agents" and the hot rays of the sun. Fredrika Bremer observed them everywhere during her two-year tour of the United States. Writing in the spring of 1850 from a home along the Hudson River, she reported, "Here, as in many other places, I observed how they exclude the daylight from the rooms. This troubles me, who am accustomed to our light rooms in Sweden, and who love the light. But they say that the heat of the sun is too powerful here for the greater part of the year, and that they are obliged as much as possible to exclude its light from the rooms." Bremer was describing a practice that often drew comment from foreign visitors who failed to appreciate that New York City and Rome share the same latitude, as do New Orleans and Cairo. While spending the following July in Washington, D.C., even Bremer conceded that in her room "all is kept cool by the green Venetian shutters."[39]

Nor was Fredrika Bremer the only foreign visitor to

PLATE 114. *Window bays are also commonly embellished with recessed panels that may be picked out. Simple recesses* (above left) *allow for the reintroduction of the body color or a shade of the trim color. More complex compositions* (above right) *may be picked out by reversing colors more than once, rarely by introducing a third color. When painting panels in only two colors, the rule is that the moldings belong in the framing color.*

PLATE 115. *Although much faded, this late-nineteenth-century photograph of the Suggett House (1882) in Cortland, New York, clearly illustrates full picking out of the porches and bay windows. Of particular interest is the use of the body color on the quarter-round molding of the otherwise monochromatic main cornice.* Photograph courtesy of the Cortland County Historical Society

PLATE 116. *The 1882 Suggett House in Cortland, New York, in its recent brown-and-yellow paint scheme. Ironically, this historical treatment is more conservative than the original shown in Plate 115.*

PLATE 117. *A modest, attractive village house painted in Downing colors—complete with dark green shutters.*

PLATE 118. *Handsome painting of round-headed shutters that were improperly rehung on the window frames.*

comment on the American habit of painting shutters green. In the winter of 1842, the celebrated English novelist Charles Dickens traveled to America, reaching Worcester, Massachusetts, in early February. "All the buildings," he later wrote, "looked as if they had been painted that morning. . . . Every house is the whitest of white; every Venetian blind is the greenest of green." That same year, Andrew Jackson Downing published his polemic against white houses trimmed in green. "To render the effect still worse," he remarked, "our modern builders paint their venetian window shutters a bright green! A cool dark green would be in better taste, and more agreeable to the eye."[40]

If American architects, critics, and paint manufacturers were in agreement on anything it was that their countrymen loved green shutters. William H. Ranlett specified "bronze or Paris green" shutters in the 1840s and forty years later Charles L. Condit and Jacob Scheller could still write in *Painting and Painters' Materials* that "green is the most satisfactory color" for shutters. Some paint companies even supplied ready-mixed colors specifically for this use. One manufacturer wrote, "Green is by far the most popular color for blinds. . . . In Acme Quality House Paint we offer 'Window Blind Green' to meet the demand for this popular color." Park Lawn Green was one of the first ready-mixed paint colors packaged by F. W. Devoe & Company in 1869 for "use on Window Blinds, Ornamental Iron Work, Machinery, etc." A substitute for Paris Green—an extremely poisonous color made from green arsenic pigment—Park Lawn Green was created by mixing yellow and blue pigments and came in light, medium, and dark shades.[41]

According to Condit and Scheller, if ever-popular green happened not to be "harmonious with the chosen house color, it is, perhaps, better to keep very near

(darker or lighter) to the house color. . . ." Calvert Vaux, formerly an associate of Downing's, also recommended this darker or lighter use of the trim or body color as an acceptable alternative. If the shutters were painted the *same* color as the house, he warned, "a blank, uninteresting effect will be produced, for when the blinds are closed, which is generally the case, the house, except to a person very near to it, will appear to be without any windows at all."[42]

A few surviving specifications from the nineteenth century do suggest alternative treatments, particularly those where *two* colors are to be applied. As early as 1833, James Gallier confirmed this practice by noting in the *American Builder's General Price Book and Estimator* that "party" color painting of shutters—meaning that the rails and panels (or louvers) are different colors—cost more "for the trouble incurred by applying two colors." Occasionally shutters are found painted in the trim color of the house with the recessed panels or louvers picked out in the body color, or in an even darker shade of the body-trim combination. In 1886 the manufacturer of Breinig's Ready Mixed Paints stated, "Where the blinds are painted the same color as the house, a pleasing effect is obtained by painting the slats with the trimming color and the frame of the blinds with the body color."[43]

As a general historical rule, shutters should be:

1. Painted green, with preference for dark green that may even appear nearly black, or
2. Painted a lighter or darker shade of the house color with preference for the darker, or
3. Picked out in two colors: either body and trim or lighter or darker shades of the body or trim colors.

Darker shades are favored for shutters in order to continue the visual concept of the window void when the shutters are closed.

Keep in mind that to be practical, shutters must shut. Do not fix your exterior shutters permanently in the open position. (One sees this too often today, particularly with the molded plastic or pressed metal types sold in most cash-and-carry building-supply stores. And even if these shutters were to be closed, they are often the wrong size and would not properly cover the windows.) In addition, many nineteenth-century houses used solid panel shutters on the ground floor—for security—and louvered shutters above that level for ventilation. This is a distinction too often overlooked when fitting Victorian houses with replacement shutters. Last, be sure not to install your louvered shutters backward; they should be placed so that when closed over the window during a rainstorm, the slant of the louvers will direct the rain away from, rather than into, the interior of the house.

PLATE 119. *Picking out of shutter louvers and panels on a vernacular frame house of c. 1880. Notice also the sandwich brackets and the porch post detailing.*

DOORS

Depending upon their age and material, the doors of Victorian buildings are usually finished by 1) painting in the trim color or a combination of trim and body colors, 2) graining to simulate a hard wood, or 3) staining and varnishing to display the natural wood grain.

Painted Doors

The majority of soft wood exterior doors appear to have been painted. In their 1884 promotional book *House Painting* the Sherwin-Williams Company counseled: "Where the outside doors are to be painted, use some contrasting color that will harmonize with the color of the house, or a very good effect is obtained by painting with the same colors used on the house—the darkest color for the sunken panels and the medium or next lighter color for the stiles." Most critics also recommended that the door *frames* be painted in the principal trim color used around windows.[44]

Grained Doors

Soft wood exterior doors could also be grained to simulate more expensive woods such as oak or mahogany. In the nineteenth century every master housepainter could grain, and the use of this decorative technique was common; but gradually the skill was lost. Fortunately, the modern demand for graining has encouraged some painters to learn the technique, so you can usually locate someone to regrain your doors.

Graining is executed over a base of oil paint applied directly to the sanded and primed surface. The color of the base is determined by the wood being imitated. Ash, maple, birch, and oak—all popular graining choices in the nineteenth century—are light woods and hence ap-

PLATE 120. *N. B. Van Slyke sketched his new cottage at Maple Bluff, Wisconsin, and described it as "painted something like this. Body White (in the natural woods of large Elm, Maple, Butternut and Basswood trees.) Trimmings, grass green; shingling the natural color of new pine wood. Roof vermillion. . . ." Although the white body is fully outlined in the green trim, the board shutters are white and there is no picking out of the porch decoration or lattice—altogether a conservative paint scheme. Fortunately a black-and-white photograph of the cottage also survives from 1884 (below). Photograph courtesy of the State Historical Society of Wisconsin*

plied over yellowish white bases. Walnut, another popular choice, is applied over an orangey base, while mahogany requires a reddish base. The graining glaze, unlike the base coat of paint, is semitransparent and allows the base coat to show through as the lighter areas of the grain. A layer of varnish, laid over the finished surface to protect it, must be renewed every year or two, especially on exterior surfaces.[45]

The relative thickness of these three coats causes confusion for many owners or curators of old houses when they scrape small sections of woodwork. Suddenly a base coat of yellowish white or orange appears that is taken to have been the finish color of the original woodwork. While this is possible—and only a microanalysis would determine for sure—it is more probably the base coat for graining. Since the graining coat (glaze) itself is quite thin, evidence of its presence under later paint is fugitive at best.

Surviving examples suggest that the frames of grained doors were often painted in the trimming color. If evidence of graining is found, you should restore the graining, or at least paint the door in a semigloss oil paint in a color as close to the original graining glaze as is possible. (In some cases where regraining has not been possible, we have recommended painting the doors a deep reddish brown; from a distance this color will "read" as if the doors were grained.) However, graining is relatively easy to do and there is little real justification for not regraining if the original treatment cannot be saved by carefully removing later overpainting.

Graining gradually fell from favor in the late nineteenth century as stained and varnished hardwood doors became popular. One author complained in the 1880s,

A great many outside doors are still grained in imitation of natural woods, which is a very great detriment to the advancement of artistic exteriors, because, in the first place, it is in very poor taste, and is an imitation and deception, and all imitations are bad; in the next place, it gives rise to more bad feeling and dissatisfaction than any other work performed, for it is almost impossible to find a door that has been grained that will stand the sun and weather without blistering and cracking. The graining color comes off in round spots, exposing the light color underneath, producing a very unsightly appearance. When a door becomes spotted in this way the thing generally thought of is to remove the old graining and finish as before, which is very unsatisfactory and expensive to the owner, as it will blister and come off again.

Unfortunately, these criticisms have some validity. If the varnish coat is not renewed regularly the graining will fail. However, the front doors of The Athenaeum

of Philadelphia (Plate 121) were regrained over a decade ago and have suffered no losses because they are revarnished regularly.[46]

Hardwood Doors

It is rare to find an exterior door made of hardwood that was not originally intended to be stained and varnished. Unfortunately, many of these have obtained later coatings of paint, usually several coats of white enamel. The quickest way to check for hardwoods is to scrape through the layers of paint on one of the narrow edges of the door to expose the grain of the wood. Alternatively, removing some hardware may expose a small patch of original finish—any vandal who would paint over a hardwood door will probably have been too lazy to remove the hardware before painting. Nineteenth-century painters always finished doors before mounting key and bellpull escutcheons, doorknob back plates, and mail slot covers. This trick, by the way, also works as a quick check for original paint colors and graining.[47]

The refinishing of exterior hardwood doors differs little from the process used for furniture except that the final protective coating is an exterior grade varnish. If you are uncertain about the stripping, preparation, and staining of hardwoods, we recommend you read George Grotz's *The Furniture Doctor* (Garden City, New York: Doubleday & Company, 1962). This irreverent classic is filled with helpful hints. Also, the warning about maintaining a good varnish coat to preserve graining is true for natural-finish doors too—the varnish must be renewed every year or two, depending upon the severity of the climate and the exposure the door suffers.

Hardware

It is impossible to refinish a door well—whether painted, grained, or varnished—without removing all the metal hardware. While it is off the door the hardware should be cleaned of all paint and varnish by soaking overnight in a good-quality paint stripper. Usually the hardware will be brass or bronze and should be polished and relacquered before being returned to the door. Painters are rarely patient enough to clean hardware thoroughly, so you may have to do it yourself with metal polish and 0000 steel wool, or you can take it to a local metal refinisher.

This is also a good time to remove and consign to the

PLATE 121. *Grained doors as restored in 1975 at The Athenaeum of Philadelphia, Malcolm Robson, grainer, Fairfax, Virginia.* Photograph courtesy of The Athenaeum of Philadelphia

trash any plastic or cast-iron eagles, cute mailboxes with broken-pediment tops, nameplates cunningly shaped like lampposts or horse-drawn carriages, and plastic or reflector-tape house numbers that previous owners may have installed. Such hardware-store kitsch has no more place on a Victorian house than do front-yard embellishments like truck tire planters painted silver, plastic pink flamingos, or earthenware figurines of serape-clad boys leading donkeys.

Storm and Screen Doors

Nothing spoils the look of a carefully painted doorway more than a white or natural aluminum screen or storm door of the type designed for mobile homes and inexpensive development houses. If you are fortunate enough to have the original screen doors for your house they should be renovated and painted the same color as the all-weather doors. If you need new screen door frames, there are several firms manufacturing handsome wooden ones in a variety of Victorian patterns (for addresses, check *The Old-House Journal Catalog* published periodically by *The Old-House Journal*, 69A Seventh Avenue, Brooklyn, New York 11217). Storm doors are more difficult. The most satisfactory solution we have found is a custom-made *wooden* storm door with a relatively small frame that allows the all-weather door to show through the glass.

APPENDIX

Paint Failure and Surface Preparation

No matter how carefully you have studied color choice and worked out color placement and finishes, your repainting will fail if the surface is not properly prepared in advance. Too often, however, this preparation involves removal of old finishes. In the process of removing old finishes, the underlying surfaces—especially wood—can be damaged, historical color documentation can be destroyed, and you or your painter may be exposed to the toxic effects of lead, which was commonly used in pre–World War II paints.

Fortunately, the Preservation Assistance Divison of the National Park Service, U.S. Department of the Interior, has prepared a "Preservation Brief" on this topic written by Kay D. Weeks and David W. Look, AIA, and published in 1982. This is simply the best short essay on the subject we have ever found, and it should be read by every historical building owner prior to repainting. The following remarks are excerpted from this *Preservation Brief 10* with the kind permission of Lee H. Nelson, AIA, Chief, Preservation Assistance Division. Copies of the full report are available from the Superintendent of Documents, U.S. Government Printing Office, Washington, D.C. 20402.

IDENTIFICATION OF EXTERIOR PAINT SURFACE CONDITIONS/ RECOMMENDED TREATMENTS

Paint surface conditions can be grouped according to their relative severity: Class I conditions include minor blemishes or dirt collection and generally require *no* paint removal; Class II conditions include failure of the top layer or layers of paint and generally require *limited* paint removal; and Class III conditions include substantial or multiple-layer failure and generally require *total* paint removal. It is precisely because conditions will vary at different points on the buildings that a careful inspection is critical. Each item of painted exterior woodwork (i.e, siding, doors, windows, eaves, shutters, and decorative elements) should be examined early in the planning phase and surface conditions noted.

Class I Exterior Surface Conditions Generally Requiring No Paint Removal

Dirt, Soot, Pollution, Cobwebs, Insect Cocoons, etc.

Recommended Treatment
Most surface matter can be loosened by a strong, direct stream of water from the nozzle of a garden hose. Stubborn dirt and soot will need to be scrubbed off using 1/2 cup of household detergent in a gallon of water with a medium soft bristle brush. The cleaned surface should then be rinsed thoroughly, and permitted to dry before further inspection to determine if repainting is necessary. Quite often, cleaning provides a satisfactory enough result to postpone repainting.

Mildew

Recommended Treatment
Because mildew can only exist in shady, warm, moist areas, attention should be given to altering the environment that is conducive to fungal growth. The area in question may be shaded by trees that need to be pruned back to allow sunlight to strike the building; or may lack rain gutters or proper drainage at the base of the building. If the shady or moist conditions can be altered, the mildew is less likely to reappear. A rec-

ommended solution for removing mildew consists of one cup nonammoniated detergent, one quart household bleach, and one gallon water. When the surface is scrubbed with this solution using a medium soft brush, the mildew should disappear; however, for particularly stubborn spots, an additional quart of bleach may be added. After the area is mildew-free, it should then be rinsed with a direct stream of water from the nozzle of a garden hose, and permitted to dry thoroughly. When repainting, specially formulated "mildew-resistant" primer and finish coats should be used.

Excessive Chalking

Recommended Treatment
The chalk should be cleaned off with a solution of $\frac{1}{2}$ cup household detergent to one gallon water, using a medium soft bristle brush. After scrubbing to remove the chalk, the surface should be rinsed with a direct stream of water from the nozzle of a garden hose, allowed to dry thoroughly (but not long enough for the chalking process to recur), and repainted, using a nonchalking paint.

Staining

Recommended Treatment
When stains are caused by rusting of the heads of nails used to attach shingles or siding to an exterior wall or by rusting or oxidizing iron, steel, or copper anchorage devices adjacent to a painted surface, the metal objects themselves should be hand sanded and coated with a rust-inhibitive primer followed by two finish coats. (Exposed nail heads should ideally be countersunk, spot primed, and the holes filled with a high-quality wood filler except where exposure of the nail head was part of the original construction system or the wood is too fragile to withstand the countersinking procedure.)

Discoloration due to color extractives in replacement wood can usually be cleaned with a solution of equal parts denatured alcohol and water. After the affected area has been rinsed and permitted to dry, a "stain-blocking primer" specially developed for preventing this type of stain should be applied (two primer coats are recommended for severe cases of bleeding prior to the finish coat). Each primer coat should be allowed to dry at least forty-eight hours.

Class II Exterior Surface Conditions Generally Requiring Limited Paint Removal

Crazing

Recommended Treatment
Crazing can be treated by hand or mechanically sanding the surface, then repainting. Although the hairline cracks may tend to show through the new paint, the surface will be protected against exterior moisture penetration.

Intercoat Peeling

Recommended Treatment
First, where salts or impurities have caused the peeling, the affected area should be washed down thoroughly after scraping, then wiped dry. Finally, the surface should be hand or mechanically sanded, then repainted.

Where peeling was the result of using incompatible paints, the peeling top coat should be scraped and hand or mechanically sanded. Application of a high-quality oil-type exterior primer will provide a surface over which either an oil or a latex top coat can be successfully used.

Solvent Blistering

Recommended Treatment
Solvent-blistered areas can be scraped, hand or mechanically sanded to the next sound layer, then repainted. In order to prevent blistering of painted surfaces, paint should not be applied in direct sunlight.

Wrinkling

Recommended Treatment
The wrinkled layer can be removed by scraping followed by hand or mechanical sanding to provide as even a surface as possible, then repainted following manufacturer's application instructions.

Class III Exterior Surface Conditions Generally Requiring Total Paint Removal

If surface conditions are such that the majority of paint will have to be removed prior to repainting, it is suggested that a small sample of intact paint be left in an inconspicuous area either by covering the area with a metal plate or by marking the area and identifying it in some way. (When repainting does take place, the sample should not be painted over.) This will enable future investigators to have a record of the building's paint history.

Peeling

Recommended Treatment
There is no sense in repainting before dealing with the moisture problems because new paint will simply fail. Therefore, the first step in treating peeling is to locate and remove the source or sources of the moisture, not only because moisture will jeopardize the protective coating of paint but because, if left unattended, it can ultimately cause permanent damage to the wood. Excess interior moisture should be removed from the building through installation of exhaust fans and vents. Exterior moisture should be eliminated by correcting the following conditions prior to repainting: faulty flashing; leaking gutters; defective roof shingles; cracks and holes in siding and trim; deteriorated caulking in joints and seams; and shrubbery growing too close to painted wood. After the moisture problems have been solved, the wood must be permitted to dry out thoroughly. The damaged paint can then be scraped off with a putty knife, hand or mechanically sanded, primed, and repainted.

Cracking/Alligatoring

Recommended Treatment
If cracking and alligatoring are present only in the top layers they can probably be scraped, hand or mechanically sanded to the next sound layer, then repainted. However, if cracking and/or alligatoring have progressed to bare wood and the paint

has begun to flake, it will need to be totally removed. Methods include scraping or paint removal with the electric heat plate, electric heat gun, or chemical strippers, depending on the particular area involved. Bare wood should be primed within forty-eight hours, then repainted.

SELECTING THE APPROPRIATE/ SAFEST METHOD TO REMOVE PAINT

After having presented the "hierarchy" of exterior paint surface conditions—from a mild condition such as mildewing, which simply requires cleaning prior to repainting, to serious conditions such as peeling and alligatoring, which require total paint removal—one important thought bears repeating: if a paint problem has been identified that warrants either limited or total paint removal, the gentlest method possible for the particular wooden element of the historic building should be selected from the many available methods.

The treatments recommended—based upon field testing as well as on-site monitoring of Department of Interior grant-in-aid and certification of rehabilitation projects—are therefore those which take three overriding issues into consideration: (1) the continued protection and preservation of the historic exterior woodwork; (2) the retention of the sequence of historic paint layers; and (3) the health and safety of those individuals performing the paint removal. By applying these criteria, it will be seen that no paint removal method is without its drawbacks and all recommendations are qualified in varying degrees.

Abrasive Methods (Manual)

If conditions have been identified that require limited paint removal such as crazing, intercoat peeling, solvent blistering, and wrinkling, scraping and hand sanding should be the first methods employed before using mechanical means. Even in the case of more serious conditions such as peeling—where the damaged paint is weak and already sufficiently loosened from the wood surface—scraping and hand sanding may be all that is needed prior to repainting.

Summary of Abrasive Methods (Manual)

Recommended: Putty knife, paint scraper, sandpaper, sanding block, sanding sponge.
Applicable areas of building: All areas.
For use on: Class I, Class II, and Class III conditions.
Health/Safety factors: Take precautions against lead dust, eye damage; dispose of lead paint residue properly.

Abrasive Methods (Mechanical)

If hand sanding for purposes of surface preparation has not been productive or if the affected area is too large to consider hand sanding by itself, mechanical abrasive methods, i.e., power-operated tools, may need to be employed; however, it should be noted that the majority of tools available for paint removal can cause damage to fragile wood and must be used with great care.

Summary of Abrasive Methods (Mechanical)

Recommended: Orbital sander, belt sander (skilled operator only).
Applicable areas of building: Flat surfaces, i.e., siding, eaves, doors, windowsills.
For use on: Class II and Class III conditions.
Health/Safety factors: Take precautions against lead dust and eye damage; dispose of lead paint residue properly.
Not Recommended: Rotary drill attachments, high-pressure waterblasting, sandblasting.

Thermal Methods

Where exterior surface conditions have been identified that warrant total paint removal such as peeling, cracking, or alligatoring, two thermal devices—the electric heat plate and the electric heat gun—have proven to be quite successful for use on different wooden elements of the historic building. One thermal method—the blow torch—is not recommended because it can scorch the wood or even burn the building down!

Summary of Thermal Methods

Recommended: Electric heat plate, electric heat gun.
Applicable areas of building: Electric heat plate—flat surfaces such as siding, eaves, sash, sills, doors. Electric heat gun—solid decorative molding, balusters, fretwork, or "gingerbread."
For use on: Class III conditions.
Health/Safety factors: Take precautions against eye damage and fire. Dispose of lead paint residue properly.
Not Recommended: Blow torch.

Chemical Methods

With the availability of effective thermal methods for total paint removal, the need for chemical methods—in the context of preparing historic exterior woodwork for repainting—becomes quite limited. Solvent-base or caustic strippers may, however, play a supplemental role in a number of situations, including:

- Removing paint residue from intricate decorative features, or in cracks or hard-to-reach areas if a heat gun has not been completely effective;
- Removing paint on window muntins because heat devices can easily break the glass;
- Removing varnish on exterior doors after all layers of paint have been removed by a heat plate/heat gun if the original varnish finish is being restored;
- Removing paint from detachable wooden elements such as exterior shutters, balusters, columns, and doors by dip-stripping when other methods are too laborious.

Summary of Chemical Methods

Recommended, with extreme caution: Solvent-base strippers, caustic strippers.
Applicable areas of buildings: Decorative features, window muntins, doors, exterior shutters, columns, balusters, and railings.
For use on: Class III conditions.

Health/Safety factors: Take precautions against inhaling toxic vapors; fire; eye damage; and chemical poisoning from skin contact. Dispose of lead residue properly.

GENERAL PAINT TYPE RECOMMENDATIONS

Based on the assumption that the exterior wood has been painted with oil paint many times in the past and the existing top coat is therefore also an oil paint,* it is recommended that for Class I and Class II paint surface conditions, a top coat of high-quality oil paint be applied when repainting. The reason for recommending oil rather than latex paints is that a coat of latex paint applied directly over old oil paint is more apt to fail. The considerations are twofold. First, because oil paints continue to harden with age, the old surface is sensitive to the added stress of shrinkage that occurs as a new coat of paint dries. Oil paints shrink less upon drying than latex paints and thus do not have as great a tendency to pull the old paint loose. Second, when exterior oil paints age, the binder releases pigment particles, causing a chalky surface. Although for best results, the chalk (or dirt, etc.) should *always* be cleaned off prior to repainting, a coat of new oil paint is more able to penetrate a chalky residue and adhere than is latex paint. Therefore, unless it is possible to thoroughly clean a heavy chalked surface, oil paints—on balance—give better adhesion.

If, however, a latex top coat is going to be applied over several layers of old oil paint, an oil primer should be applied first (the oil primer creates a flat, porous surface to which the latex can adhere). After the primer has thoroughly dried, a latex top coat may be applied. In the long run, changing paint types is more time-consuming and expensive. An application of a new oil-type top coat on the old oil paint is, thus, the preferred course of action.

If Class III conditions have necessitated total paint removal, there are two options, both of which assure protection of the exterior wood: (1) an oil primer may be applied followed by an oil-type top coat, preferably by the same manufacturer; or (2) an oil primer may be applied followed by a latex top coat, again using the same brand of paint. It should also be noted that primers were never intended to withstand the effects of weathering; therefore, the top coat should be applied as soon as possible after the primer has dried.

CONCLUSION

The recommendations outlined in this brief are cautious because at present there is no completely safe and effective method of removing old paint from exterior woodwork. This has necessarily eliminated descriptions of several methods still in a developmental or experimental stage, which can therefore be neither recommended nor precluded from future recommendation. With the ever-increasing number of buildings being rehabilitated, however, paint removal technology should be stimulated and, in consequence, existing methods refined and new methods developed that will respect both the historic wood and the health and safety of the operator.

*If the top coat is latex paint (when viewed by the naked eye or, preferably, with a magnifying glass, it looks like a series of tiny craters) it may either be repainted with new latex paint or with oil paint. Normal surface preparation should precede any repainting.

PICTORIAL GLOSSARY

Numbers are keyed to all three drawings of this Victorian architectural glossary, from Color Applied to Architecture *(Cleveland: Sherwin-Williams Company, 1887).* The Athenaeum of Philadelphia Collection

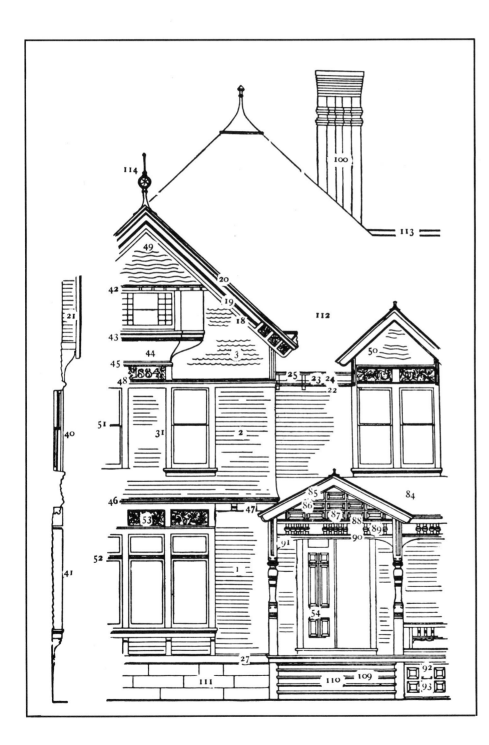

1.–3. Body
  1. First story
  2. Second story
  3. Attic
4.–25. Cornice
  4. Edge of crown mold
  5. Crown
  6. Fascia
  7. Bed mold
  8. Dentals
  9. Frieze
  10. Panel mold
  11. Panel
  12. Architrave
  13. Sunken face of sandwich bracket
  14. Raised face of sandwich bracket
  15. Bracket panel
  16. Bracket margin
  17. Soffit
  18.–20. Bargeboard
  21. Ceiling under eaves
  22. Foot pieces
  23. Gutter face
  24. Gutter brackets
  25. Gutter cap
26. Corner Board
27.–30. Water Table
  28. Slope
  29. Edge
  30. Face
31.–45. Window Frame or Casing
  32. Face
  33. Cap fillet
  34. Cap mold
  35. Cap panel
  36. Keystone
  37. Chamfer
  38. Sill

(continued)

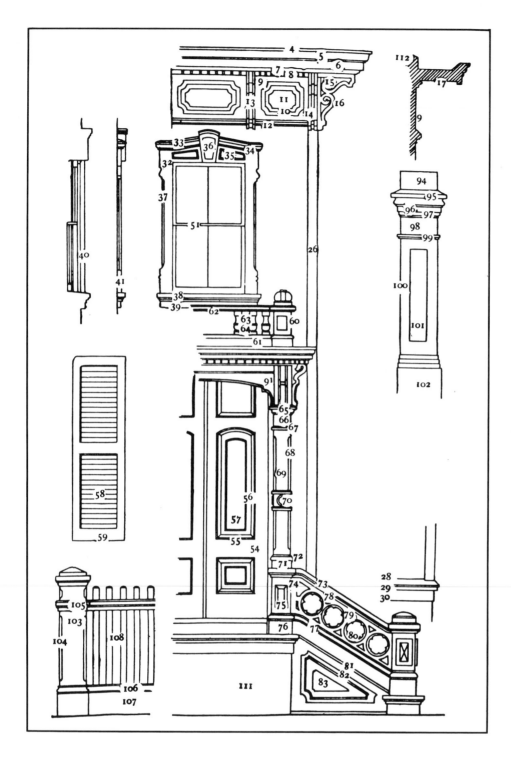

39. Apron
40. Reveal
41. Edge
42. Attic window cornice
43. Attic window sill mold
44. Attic window cove
45. Attic window base mold
46. **Belt Course**
47. **Beam Ends**
48. **Attic Belt Course**
49.–50. **Tympanum**
51. **Window Sash**
52. **Window Transom**
53. **Cut Work**
54.–57. **Doors**
54. Stiles and rails
55. Mold
56. Receding part of panel
57. Projecting part of panel
58.–59. **Shutters (Blinds)**
58. Louvers (slats)
59. Frame
60.–93. **Porch**
60. Balustrade post
61. Balustrade base
62. Balustrade rail
63. Receding part of baluster
64. Projecting part of baluster
65. Abacus
66. Capital
67. Neck mold
68. Chamfer
69. Shaft
70. Rosette
71. Plinth
72. Plinth mold
73. Rail
74. Dado
75. Dado panel
76. Base

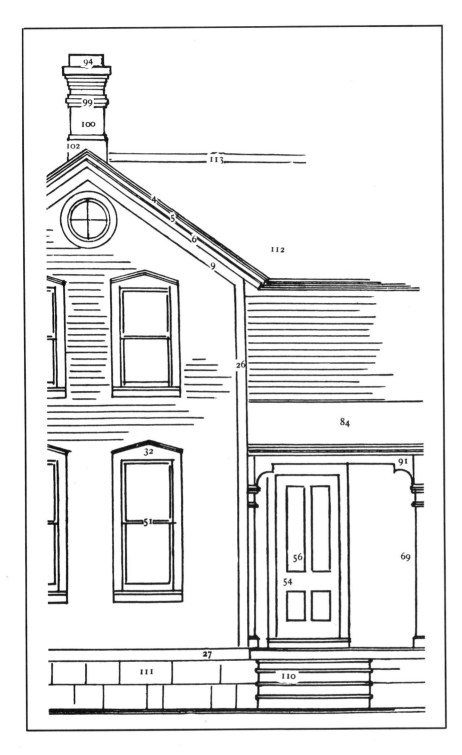

77. Base mold
78. Ornamental rail
79. Ornamental panel
80. Ornamental chamfer
81. Bead below steps
82. Panel mold below steps
83. Panel below steps
84. Roof
85. Face rafter (bargeboard)
86. Gable rail
87. Gable panels
88. Plate
89. Cornice balusters
90. Cornice rail
91. Cornice bracket
92. Rails below
93. Panels below

94.–102. Chimney
94. Top of cap
95. Crown mold of cap
96. Fascia of cap
97. Bed mold of cap
98. Frieze of cap
99. Architrave
100. Shaft
101. Panels
102. Base

103.–108. Fence
103. Post
104. Post chamfer
105. Upper rail
106. Lower rail
107. Base
108. Pickets (balusters)

109.–110. Steps
109. Tread mold
110. Riser

111. Foundation

112.–114. Roof
113. Ridge roll or cresting
114. Iron finials (also common location for acroterion)

NOTES

Introduction

1. Samuel Sloan, *The Model Architect* (Philadelphia, 1852), vol. 2, pp. 77–78.
2. Ehrick Kensett Rossiter and Frank Ayers Wright, *Modern House Painting* (New York, 1882), p. 7. Fear of colors other than white continues to be an issue with the uninformed. See William E. Geist, "In Litchfield, Hue and Cry for Tradition," *New York Times*, Dec. 3, 1982, and Roger W. Moss, "A Place for Color in the Tradition of U.S. Houses," *New York Times*, Dec. 18, 1982.

1 How Authentic Must My Paint Scheme Be?

1. For a detailed discussion of the Scientific approach, see Carole L. Perrault, "Techniques Employed at the North Atlantic Historic Preservation Center for Sampling and Analysis of Historic Architectural Paints and Finishes," *Bulletin of the Association for Preservation Technology* 10, no. 2 (1978), pp. 6–46. For a bibliography of useful articles on the Scientific approach, see also Frank S. Welsh, "Paint Analysis," *Bulletin of the Association for Preservation Technology* 14, no. 4 (1982), pp. 29–30.
2. Morgan W. Phillips, "Problems in the Restoration and Preservation of Old House Paints," in *Preservation and Conservation: Principles and Practices*, Sharon Timmons ed. (Washington, D.C.: Preservation Press, 1976), pp. 273–86.
3. *The Secretary of the Interior's Standards for Historic Preservation Projects with Guidelines for Applying the Standards* (Washington, D.C., 1979; rev., 1983) recommends

approaches on paints and finishes within various types of project work treatments.
4. *Painting and Decorating* 8, no. 3 (Dec. 1892), p. 252. Elizabeth Pomada and Michael Larson, *Painted Ladies: San Francisco's Resplendent Victorians* (New York: E. P. Dutton, 1978).
5. *How to Make Your Home Attractive* (Dayton: Lowe Brothers Paint Company, 1914). *California Architects and Builders News* (Apr. 1885), quoted in Pomada and Larson, *Painted Ladies*, p. 9. For a balanced discussion of the differences between the Boutique and the Historical approaches to painting Victorian buildings, including interviews with proponents of each, see "The Saga of the Painted Ladies," *Qualified Remodeler* 2, no. 8 (Aug. 1985), pp. 34–49.

2 Colorful Victorians, 1840–1900

1. The Averill Chemical Paint Company was issued a patent for ready-mixed paint on July 16, 1867. D. R. Averill's "patent" paint, however, was not popular, because the pigments were improperly mixed and tended to sink in the can, causing the paint to streak when applied. This problem was not overcome until 1876 when Henry A. Sherwin invented a new paint-grinding mill. Roger W. Moss, *Century of Color* (Watkins Glen, N.Y.: American Life Foundation, 1981), p. 11. For a detailed discussion of the forces at work on residential architecture, see David P. Handlin, *The American Home: Architecture and Society, 1815–1915* (Boston: Little, Brown, 1979).
2. U.S. Bureau of the Census, *Statistical Abstract of the United States*, 77th ed. (Washington, D.C., 1956), section 1.

3. For a listing of the hundreds of architectural books published in America, see Henry-Russell Hitchcock, *American Architectural Books* (reprint, New York: Da Capo Press, 1976), and on trade catalogues see Lawrence B. Romaine, *A Guide to American Trade Catalogs, 1744–1900* (New York: R. R. Bowker Company, 1960; Arno Press, 1976).

4. Richard M. Candee, "Preparing and Mixing Colors in 1812," *The Magazine Antiques* 113 (Apr. 1978), pp. 849–53, reproduces Reynolds's entire pamphlet.

5. Andrew Jackson Downing, *Cottage Residences* (New York, 1842), pp. 22–23.

6. Andrew Jackson Downing, *The Architecture of Country Houses* (New York, 1850), pp. 198–206.

7. For a review of Cooper's views on "The Color of Buildings in Rural Scenery," see the *Horticulturist* magazine for Jan. 1852, pp. 15–17. Calvert Vaux, *Villas and Cottages* (New York, 1857), pp. 54–55.

8. Downing, *Country Houses*, pp. 198–206.

9. Arthur Channing Downs, "Downing's Newburgh Villa," *Bulletin of the Association for Preservation Technology* 4, nos. 3–4 (1972), pp. 30–41, discusses the influences of Lugar and Goodwin on Downing. Downing, *Country Houses*, p. 203, lists the following "shades for outside painting": Fawn, Drab, Gray Stone, Brown Stone, French Gray, Slate, Sage, Straw, and Chocolate. C. W. Elliott, *Cottages and Cottage Life* (Cincinnati, 1848), p. 210.

10. For a bibliography of nineteenth-century sources that discuss paint, see Samuel J. Dornsife, ed., *Exterior Decoration* (Philadelphia: The Athenaeum of Philadelphia, 1976), pp. 8–16. The Devoe quotation is also from *Exterior Decoration*, pp. 18–19.

11. John Riddell, *Architectural Designs for Model Country Residences* (Philadelphia, 1861, 1864, and 1867). His book is one of the most handsome American works of architecture published in the nineteenth century. For a discussion of Riddell, see Sandra L. Tatman and Roger W. Moss, *Biographical Dictionary of Philadelphia Architects, 1700–1930* (Boston: G. K. Hall, 1985), pp. 659–62.

12. John W. Masury, *House-painting: Plain and Decorative* (New York, 1868), pp. 166–67.

13. Hay's work is cited in the following sources: John Claudius Loudon, *Encyclopedia of Cottage, Farm, and Villa Architecture and Furniture* (London, 1833; New York, 1849; reprint, 1869), p. 1274; Downing, *Country Houses*, pp. 400–402; "Art in Common Things," *Godey's Lady's Book* 79 (Aug. 1869), pp. 131–32; and Masury, *House-painting*, pp. 170–72.

14. For details see Michel Eugène Chevreul, *The Principles of Harmony and Contrast of Colors and Their Applications to the Arts* (New York: Van Nostrand Reinhold, 1967; based on the first English edition, 1854, and trans. from the first French edition, 1839). *House Painting and Decorating* 1 (Nov. 1885), pp. 41–46.

15. Chevreul, *Principles*, p. 90.

16. C. P. Sherwood, *A Few Words About Paint and Painting* (Wadsworth, Martinez & Longman, c. 1884). *House Painting and Decorating* 1 (Nov. 1885), pp. 41–46.

17. Isaac H. Hobbs, *Hobbs' Architecture*, 2nd ed. (Philadelphia, 1876), p. 150. Henry Hudson Holly, *Modern Dwellings in Town and Country* (New York, 1878), p. 27.

18. Holly, *Modern Dwellings*, p. 26.

19. *Every Man His Own Painter! or, Paints—How to Select and Use Them* (Philadelphia, 1873), p. 6. Dornsife, ed., *Exterior Decoration*, p. 19.

20. Ehrick Kensett Rossiter and Frank Ayers Wright, *Modern House Painting* (New York, 1882), pp. 6–7. H. W. Johns Company, *Structural Decoration* (1884), p. 6.

21. H. W. Johns Company, *Suggestions for Exterior Decoration* (1893), pp. 2–3.

22. Lowe Brothers Paint Company, *The House Outside & Inside: How to Make Your Home Attractive* (Dayton, 1914).

3 Selecting Colors for Victorian Buildings

1. Calvert Vaux, *Villas and Cottages* (New York, 1857), p. 57.

4 Color Placement on Victorian Buildings

1. Diana S. Waite, "Roofing for Early America," in *Building Early America*, Charles E. Peterson, ed. (Radnor, Pa.: Chilton Book Company, 1976), pp. 135–49. Philip C. Marshall, "Polychromatic Roofing Slate of Vermont and New York," *Bulletin of the Association for Preservation Technology* 11, no. 3 (1979), pp. 77–87.

2. Harley J. McKee, "Slate Roofing," *Bulletin of the Association for Preservation Technology* 2, nos. 1–2 (1970), pp. 77–84.

3. "Slate Roofs," *The Old-House Journal* 8 (May 1980), pp. 49–55. For a useful primer on traditional roofing materials see "Special Roof Issue," *The Old-House Journal* 11 (Apr. 1983), pp. 53–76. Vermont Structural Slate Company, *Slate Roofs* (1926; reprint, Fair Haven, Vt., 1977). In 1857 Calvert Vaux wrote: "Lately, new American quarries, supplying slate of different colors, have been opened in various parts of the country, and worked to success. . . . This slate, when arranged on a roof in stripes or patterns, so that the colors are equally represented, has a very agreeable effect, and one that is far superior to that produced by any shingle or metal roof." Calvert Vaux, *Villas and Cottages* (New York, 1857), p. 61.

4. C. R. Meyer, "Roofing With Wood Shingles," *The Old-House Journal* 5 (Aug. 1977), pp. 85, 93–95. Sherwin, Williams & Co., *House Painting* (Cleveland, 1884), p. 18. Ehrick Kensett Rossiter and Frank Ayers Wright, *Modern House Painting* (New York, 1882; reprint, 1883), plate 3. National Lead Company, *The House We Live In* (New York, c. 1920), p. 5.

5. Waite, "Roofing," p. 148n. Walter Jowers, "Standing Seam Roofs," *The Old-House Journal* 13 (Mar. 1985), pp. 35, 44–48.

6. John W. Masury, *How Shall We Paint Our Houses?* (New York, 1868), p. 36.

7. Paint companies well into the twentieth century rec-

ognized the need for dark roofs. The National Lead Company declared in 1920, "The roofs of bungalows are nearly always in strong, dark colors—venetian red and olive green for instance." National Lead Company, *The House We Live In*, p. 5.

8. Samuel Sloan, *The Model Architect* (Philadelphia, 1852), vol. 2, p. 85.

9. Constance M. Greiff, *John Notman, Architect* (Philadelphia: The Athenaeum of Philadelphia, 1979), pp. 152–57. John Riddell, *Architectural Designs for Model Country Residences* (Philadelphia, 1861; 2nd ed., 1864). Alexander Jackson Davis, *Rural Residences* (New York, 1837), n.p.

10. *Villas on the Hudson* (New York, c. 1860), p. 10.

11. J. Randall Cotton, "Return to Awnings," *The Old-House Journal* 13 (July 1985), pp. 115, 126–130.

12. O. C. Harn, *Correct Color Schemes* (Pittsburgh: National Lead Company, 1910), p. 9.

13. Roger W. Moss, *Century of Color* (Watkins Glen, N.Y.: American Life Foundation, 1981), p. 103.

14. John C. Fitzpatrick, ed., *The Writings of George Washington* (Washington, D.C.: Government Printing Office, 1940), vol. 37, pp. 386–87. F. S. Welsh and C. L. Granquist, "Restoration of the Exterior Sanded Paint at Monticello," *Bulletin of the Association for Preservation Technology*, 15, no. 2 (1983), pp. 3–10.

15. Alexander Jackson Davis, *Rural Residences* (New York, 1837), specifications for a "Villa in the English Collegiate Style." Gervase Wheeler, *Rural Homes* (New York, 1851), pp. 42, 158. On Wheeler, see the essay in Sandra L. Tatman and Roger W. Moss, *Biographical Dictionary of Philadelphia Architects, 1700–1930* (Boston: G. K. Hall, 1985), pp. 849–50.

16. Andrew Jackson Downing, *The Architecture of Country Houses* (New York, 1850), p. 36n.

17. Joseph Gwilt, *Encyclopedia of Architecture* (London, 1842), p. 455.

18. Calder Loth, "A Mid-Nineteenth Century Color Scheme," *Bulletin of the Association for Preservation Technology* 9, no. 2 (1977), pp. 82–88.

19. Wheeler, *Rural Homes*, pp. 158, 209. On the painting of architectural cast iron, see Pamela Whitney Hawkes, "Paints for Architectural Cast Iron," *Bulletin of the Association for Preservation Technology* 11, no. 1 (1979), pp. 17–36. The earliest use of sand on cast iron that Hawkes discovered was 1830 by John Haviland in Pottsville, Pennsylvania.

20. Welsh and Granquist, "Restoration of Exterior Sanded Paint," pp. 3–10. Gervase Wheeler, *Homes for the People* (New York, 1855), p. 415.

21. Wheeler, *Rural Homes*, pp. 118, 39.

22. For information on the glitter gun, see *The Old-House Journal* 7 (Sept. 1979), p. 106. If granular sizes prove too large for the glitter gun, Welsh and Granquist suggest another technique that they used successfully at Monticello.

23. *Universal Moulding Book . . .* (Chicago: Rand, McNally & Company, 1871). The Athenaeum of Philadelphia owns several catalogues having different mill names that are otherwise identical. For one documented ex-ample of a local carpenter producing such decorative elements, see Wendy Rumsey, "Jigsaw Patterns in New Braunfels, Texas," *Bulletin of the Association for Preservation Technology* 9, no. 4 (1977), pp. 41–51.

24. *Paint and Painting, A Practical Treatise on the Characteristics and Properties of Breinig's Ready Mixed Paints* (Allentown, Pa.: Allentown Manufacturing Company, c. 1886), p. 18.

25. Edward Kemp, *How to Lay Out a Small Garden* (London, 1850), p. 23. Frank Jesup Scott, *Art of Beautifying Suburban Home Grounds* (New York, 1870), p. 78.

26. See Jacob Weidenmann, *Beautifying Country Homes* (1870); reprinted as *Victorian Landscape Gardening* (Watkins Glen, N.Y.: American Life Foundation, 1978).

27. Ehrick Kensett Rossiter and Frank Ayers Wright, *Modern House Painting* (New York, 1882), plate 7.

28. Larry Jones, "Lattice Work," *The Old-House Journal* 11 (Nov. 1983), pp. 193–96.

29. B. Silliman, Jr., and C. R. Goodrich, eds., *The World of Science, Art, and Industry Illustrated* (New York, 1854).

30. Rossiter and Wright, *Modern House Painting*, plate 8.

31. Lowe Brothers Company, *How to Make Your Home Attractive* (Dayton, 1914), n.p.

32. Margot Gayle, ed., *Victorian Ironwork: A Catalogue by J. B. Wickersham* (Philadelphia: The Athenaeum of Philadelphia, 1977), pp. 35–36.

33. There is some documentation for painting cast iron black. Gervase Wheeler wrote in *Rural Homes* (p. 209), "Black or bronze are the coverings for iron—the grave, honest, strengthy old substance will only be contented with sober, unchanging negation of gaiety in color."

34. *What Color?* (Cleveland: Sherwin-Williams Company, 1885), pp. 18–19.

35. *Exterior Decoration* (Philadelphia: The Athenaeum of Philadelphia, 1976; originally published by the Devoe Paint Company, 1885), p. 19.

36. Andrew Jackson Downing, *The Architecture of Country Houses* (New York, 1850), p. 204.

37. Vaux, *Villas and Cottages*, p. 56.

38. C. W. Elliot, *Cottages and Cottage Life* (Cincinnati, 1848), p. 210. *House Painting* (Cleveland: Sherwin-Williams Company, 1884), p. 17. Another manufacturer remarked that "Browns or Dark Reds may be used with good effect where warm yellows are used on buildings." *Suggestions for Exterior Decoration* (New York: H. W. Johns Manufacturing Company, 1893), p. 2. The taste for dark sash on residential structures survived until World War I, although the growing popularity of Colonial Revival structures resulted in a certain color schizophrenia: "Window sashes are usually painted black, white, Ivy Green, or deep rich colors such as copper Browns." *Acme Quality Painting Guide Book* (Detroit: Acme White Lead and Color Works, 1916), p. 21.

39. Fredrika Bremer, *The Homes of the New World* (New York, 1853), vol. 1, pp. 35, 470.

40. Charles Dickens, *American Notes for General Circulation* (London, 1874), p. 81. Andrew Jackson Downing, *Cottage Residences* (New York, 1842), p. 22n.

41. Charles L. Condit and Jacob Scheller, *Painting and*

Painters' Materials (New York, 1883), p. 403. *Acme Quality Painting Guide Book*, p. 21. "Park Lawn Green" Broadside, F. W. Devoe & Company, Spring 1869, The Athenaeum of Philadelphia Collection. Theodore Zuk Penn, "Decorative and Protective Finishes, 1750–1850," *Bulletin of the Association for Preservation Technology* 16, no. 1 (1984), pp. 15–16. Paris Green was variously known as Schweinfurt Green and Emerald Green; all variations were extremely poisonous.

42. Condit and Scheller, *Painting*, p. 403. Vaux, *Villas and Cottages*, p. 56.

43. James Gallier, *American Builder's General Price Book and Estimator* (New York, 1833), p. 118. Gallier's work was plagiarized by A. Bryant Clough in his *Contractor's Manual* (Philadelphia, 1855), including this passage. *Paint and Painting, A Practical Treatise on the Characteristics and Properties of Breinig's Ready Mixed Paints* (Allentown, Pa.: Allentown Manufacturing Company, c. 1886), p. 18.

44. *House Painting* (Cleveland: Sherwin-Williams Company, 1884), p. 18.

45. If you are tempted to learn graining yourself there are several good sources to help you: Jocasta Innes, *Paint Magic* (New York: Van Nostrand Reinhold, 1981); Isabel O'Neil, *The Art of the Painted Finish for Furniture & Decoration* (New York: William Morrow, 1971); Nat Weinstein, "The Art of Graining," *The Old-House Journal* 6 (Dec. 1978), pp. 133ff, and 7 (Jan. 1979), pp. 5ff. For a more detailed discussion of graining in the Victorian house, see Gail C. Winkler and Roger W. Moss, *Victorian Interior Decoration* (New York: Henry Holt, 1986).

46. *House Painting*, p. 18.

47. If you expose the wood grain and are still in the dark, ask a friend who works with wood or obtain a copy of Herbert L. Edlin's *What Wood Is That?* (New York, 1969); this manual of wood identification contains forty actual wood samples.

INDEX

Page numbers in italics refer to illustration captions.